THE WAY OF GRATITUDE
READINGS FOR A JOYFUL LIFE

THE WAY OF GRATITUDE

READINGS FOR A JOYFUL LIFE

Michael Leach, James T. Keane,
Doris Goodnough, editors

ORBIS BOOKS
Maryknoll, New York 10545

Founded in 1970, Orbis Books endeavors to publish works that enlighten the mind, nourish the spirit, and challenge the conscience. The publishing arm of the Maryknoll Fathers and Brothers, Orbis seeks to explore the global dimensions of the Christian faith and mission, to invite dialogue with diverse cultures and religious traditions, and to serve the cause of reconciliation and peace. The books published reflect the views of their authors and do not represent the official position of the Maryknoll Society. To learn more about Maryknoll and Orbis Books, please visit our website at www.maryknollsociety.org.

Manufactured in the United States of America.
Design: Roberta Savage

Library of Congress Cataloging-in-Publication Data
Names: Leach, Michael, 1940- editor.
Title: The way of gratitude : readings for a joyful life / Michael Leach, James T. Keane, Doris Goodnough, editors.
Description: Maryknoll : Orbis Books, 2017. | Includes index.
Identifiers: LCCN 2016057897 (print) | LCCN 2017007849 (ebook) | ISBN
        9781626982321 (pbk.) | ISBN 9781608336975 (e-book)
Subjects: LCSH: Gratitude—Religious aspects—Christianity. | Gratitude.
Classification: LCC BV4647.G8 W39 2017 (print) | LCC BV4647.G8 (ebook) | DDC
        241/.4—dc23
LC record available at https://lccn.loc.gov/2016057897

Gratitude is the doorway to joy.

—Thomas Hora, M.D.

Contents

The Way of Gratitude

Contents

THE WAY OF GRATITUDE

Contents

Contents

The Way of Gratitude

Contents

The Way of Gratitude

Introduction

The Most Beautiful Words You'll Ever Hear

"I'm sorry."
"I forgive you."
"Thank you!"

"I love you."
"I love you, too. Thank you."

"This is the day the Lord has made. Let us
rejoice and be glad."
"Thank you, God, for this wonderful day!"

"Please, may I help you?"
"Yes. Thank you!"

"Thank you for your gift to the United Way
. . .
Catholic Charities . . .
Jewish Family Services . . .
Save the Children . . .
The Red Cross . . .

1

Christ Church . . .
Doctors without Borders . . .
Habitat for Humanity . . .
Your neighborhood food bank . . .
Your neighbor . . ."
"Thank *you* for the opportunity to give."

Have you ever heard these words before? Spoken them? Did your mother teach you that "Thank you" and "I love you" and "I forgive you" are among the most beautiful words you'll ever say or hear? Of all these responses to life on the move "Thank you" is the one we say the most and that moves us most. When spoken with a grateful heart it is an Open Sesame to a vault of joy, not in a cave but throughout the universe. "Thank you" is a beat that reverberates through space, ricochets off stars, and absorbs the fire of the sun as it warms our hearts and the hearts of those who hear it. Thankfulness, appreciation, gratitude—these are modes of being that guarantee us joy. "Find a place inside where there's joy," wrote the philosopher Joseph Campbell, "and the joy will burn out the pain." Wonderful thing, we don't need to find joy. Joy finds us. Whenever we are grateful.

This book is a storehouse of stories, prayers, poems,

meditations, insights, experiences, and practices from some of the world's most beloved writers and other great writers you have never heard of. They have one thing in common. They open the meaning of gratitude and inspire us to practice it. This book has one purpose. To increase joy in you.

Thank you for reading *The Way of Gratitude*.

Michael Leach
James T. Keane
Doris Goodnough

Part One
The Meaning of Gratitude

The root of joy is gratefulness. It is not joy that makes us grateful; it is gratitude that makes us joyful.

—David Steindl-Rast

In the Beginning
There Was Kindness

Rowan Williams

Where do we come from? According to Genesis, we come from the decision of a God who shows endless, even alarming flexibility in arranging to stay near us, even when we show ourselves incapable of any stability in the place given us to occupy. We come from the Garden of Eden, the shortest golden age on record, where, before Adam and Eve have exchanged more than a sentence, they are caught up in the horribly recognizable fantasy of growing up and learning wisdom by magic not experience. We come from Noah's ark, where we have been stuffed into a small space in uncomfortable proximity to the rest of creation and made to face the fact that we are as vulnerable as any other inhabitant of this planet We come from Ur of the Chaldees, a stable and secure enough place which doesn't have enough room for the dangerous presence of a free God, so that we have to uproot ourselves and find a place where we can hear something other than the soothing noises of a familiar society.

Alleluia for this odd family tree. Our family traditions, it seems, are rather unexpected ones, traditions of a style of human living that is marked by constant searching and new starts. It is a tradition of relying on the invisible companion who repeatedly upsets our attempts to domesticate him and to smooth out the problems of growing up as persons or as communities. Genesis is a story of how God's purposes are revealed and worked out; but it gives very little comfort to anyone who imagines that human access to these purposes is simple or even (most of the time) remotely accurate as to God's methods and timescales.

So that an alleluia for Genesis is a thanksgiving for what makes the Bible (in spite of rather a lot of misrepresentation by believers and unbelievers alike) so powerful an enemy of the way people talk about manifest destiny and God-sanctioned historical missions. The first real mission we know about in the Bible is Abraham's. He is called to two things: he has to be an ancestor for God's people and he is called away from what he thinks is home. He has to live from a future he can't see—which is very different from living out a script that's clear and achievable.

Biblical history reveals the God who, as the philosopher said, "writes straight with crooked lines." Genesis ends with the chosen people happily abandoning the Promised Land; yet we know in retrospect that somehow this will be integrated into one story. Later on, the people demand a king, against God's plainest advice; yet the kingship will become another sign of God's promise. King David is chosen by God; but his career, subject of the longest personal saga in the whole of the Bible, is a roller coaster of failure, flight, betrayal, danger, precarious recovery, tragic frustration, a story in which supernatural intervention is hardly ever around. In the complex human emotions and uncertainties of this drama, it is God's action that is going forward, and God's company that is the one secure constant.

We love the idea of destiny. As individuals and as nations, we walk so readily into the role of God's chosen agents, as we see it. Yet when God tells us about the life of his chosen agents in the Bible, it looks so different, so much more dangerous or simply so much more like ordinary human hard work. As so often, the

Bible refuses to go along with our fantasies of guaranteed success. And at a time when religious rhetoric—from several quarters—about the mission to realize God's purpose in history is one of the things that most threatens the peace and sanity of the world, it should be a priority for Jews and Christians to witness to the Bible's firm commitment to the long perspective of God. "What would God do without me/us?" is a question that always lurks behind our enthusiasm for crusading of various kinds. It is the most deeply unbiblical question imaginable.

Humanity is all about "genesis," becoming; and the history of our religious growing up is all about becoming ourselves in the constant company of a God who is beyond all "genesis," beyond the processes of struggle and self-definition. Early Christians actually defined God as "the one who does not become" (and gave themselves a few intellectual headaches in the process). They were not complicating their thinking about God by messing around with Greek philosophy; they were just trying to be clear about why God was always there for people in the Bible story—because God was always free, never trapped in the circumstances of the "becoming" of his people. We can grow and change so radically just because God does not belong in our world of change. Our relation to God is what provides the background against which change can still add up to a single story. For God's friends and God's people, the unity of our lives doesn't come from living out a great dramatic script but from the unseen, faithful presence of God alongside us in all our developing.

Genesis sets the tone for the whole of the Bible, and we do no justice at all to our Jewish and Christian Scriptures if we try to reduce them to stories of in-fallible discernment by impeccable heroes. What we read about is how God, having called us and shown us what kind of God it is that we have to do with, then adjusts to our misunderstanding and self-will, constantly refusing to let us be trapped forever in the fantasies and the prisons we invent for ourselves. In a very important sense, all of Genesis, and all of the rest of the Bible, is really a long explanatory note to the opening affirmation—that the God of this story is the one whose utterly free decision is what lies at the origin of everything. The beginning of all our stories, and the stories of the planets and protozoa and dino-saurs, is generosity. None of this needed to be; God wanted it so, out of the impulse of love. God wanted the divine life to be shared and echoed. God wanted to generate in time and change the sort of life that is his own—capable of love and freedom and relationship. What he just is, he repeats in the processes of becoming. And for that reason, when God engages with the history of human beings, we should know that what we shall meet is generosity and faithfulness.

So when we tell this story of our origins, we cannot use it to boost our pride or self-satisfaction, and we cannot use it to sanctify a particular passing state of affairs. All our worth and solidity comes from the delight that God takes in what he has made. The value of any thing or person is simply that by existing it expresses the joy of God. And we know that this or that passing state of affairs has value in the degree to which it spurs us on our way to that life which God intends, that full share in divine joy and liberty which is the goal of creation itself.

What we most fundamentally and truly are is what our relation to God makes us. When we explore our past, retrieve our memories, it should not be to search out some primitive truth about our isolated selves that will reveal our "real" selves, as individuals or as societies. It should be to enrich our wondering recognition of an active love that was there before we even existed, before the first verse of our own particular "genesis" story. Our alleluia for Genesis is in truth an alleluia for the silence that comes before Genesis, the pregnant, overwhelming silence of divine fullness preparing to create its own echo in the abundance of a created, changing world.

IX.

Wendell Berry

I go by a field where once
I cultivated a few poor crops.
It is now covered with young trees,
for the forest that belongs here
has come back and reclaimed its own.
And I think of all the effort
I have wasted and all the time,
and of how much joy I took
in that failed work and how much
it taught me. For in so failing
I learned something of my place,
something of myself, and now
I welcome back the trees.

The Structure of Gratitude

David Brooks

I'm sometimes grumpier when I stay at a nice hotel. I have certain expectations about the service that's going to be provided. I get impatient if I have to crawl around looking for a power outlet, if the shower controls are unfathomable, if the place considers itself too fancy to put a coffee machine in each room. I'm sometimes happier at a budget motel, where my expectations are lower, and where a functioning iron is a bonus and the waffle maker in the breakfast area is a treat. This little phenomenon shows how powerfully expectations structure our moods and emotions, none more so than the beautiful emotion of gratitude.

Gratitude happens when some kindness exceeds expectations, when it is undeserved. Gratitude is a sort of laughter of the heart that comes about after some surprising kindness.

Most people feel grateful some of the time—after someone saves you from a mistake or brings you food during an illness. But some people seem grateful dispositionally. They seem thankful practically all of the time.

These people may have big ambitions, but they have preserved small anticipations. As most people get on in life and earn more status, they often get used to more respect and nicer treatment. But people with dispositional gratitude take nothing for granted. They take a beginner's thrill at a word of praise, at another's good performance or at each sunny day. These people are present-minded and hyperresponsive. This kind of dispositional gratitude is worth dissecting because it induces a mentality that stands in counterbalance to the mainstream threads of our culture.

We live in a capitalist meritocracy. This meritocracy encourages people to be self-sufficient—masters of their own fate. But people with dispositional gratitude are hyperaware of their continual dependence on others. They treasure the way they have been fashioned by parents, friends and ancestors who were in some ways their superiors. They're glad the ideal of individual autonomy is an illusion because if they were relying on themselves they'd be much worse off.

The basic logic of the capitalist meritocracy is that you get what you pay for, that you earn what you deserve. But people with dispositional gratitude are continually struck by the fact that they are given far more than they pay for—and are much richer than they deserve. Their families, schools and summer camps put far more into them than they give back. There's a lot of surplus goodness in daily life that can't be explained by the logic of equal exchange.

Capitalism encourages us to see human beings as self-interested, utility-maximizing creatures. But people with grateful dispositions are attuned to the gift economy where people are motivated by sympathy as well as self-interest. In the gift economy intention matters. We're grateful to people who tried to do us favors even when those favors didn't work out. In the gift economy imaginative empathy matters. We're grateful because some people showed they care about us more than we thought they did. We're grateful when others took an imaginative leap and put themselves in our mind, even with no benefit to themselves.

Gratitude is also a form of social glue. In the capitalist economy, debt is to be repaid to the lender. But a debt of gratitude is repaid forward, to another person who also doesn't deserve it. In this way each gift ripples outward and yokes circles of people in bonds of affection. It reminds us that a society isn't just a contract based on mutual benefit, but an organic connection based on natural sympathy—connections that are nurtured not by self-interest but by loyalty and service.

If you think that human nature is good and powerful, then you go around frustrated because the perfect society has not yet been achieved. But if you go through life believing that our reason is not that great, our individual skills are not that impressive, and our goodness is severely mottled, then you're sort of amazed life has managed to be as sweet as it is. You're grateful for all the institutions our ancestors gave us, like the Constitution and our customs, which shape us to be better than we'd otherwise be. Appreciation becomes the first political virtue and the need to perfect the gifts of others is the first political task.

We live in a capitalist meritocracy that encourages individualism and utilitarianism, ambition and pride. But this society would fall apart if not for another economy, one in which gifts surpass expectations, in which insufficiency is acknowledged and dependence celebrated.

Gratitude is the ability to see and appreciate this other almost magical economy. G. K. Chesterton wrote that "thanks are the highest form of thought, and that gratitude is happiness doubled by wonder."

People with grateful dispositions see their efforts grandly but not themselves. Life doesn't surpass their dreams but it nicely surpasses their expectations.

Thank Yous

Acknowledging the good that you already have in your life is the foundation for all abundance.
                                                    —Eckhart Tolle

Every day, think as you wake up: "Today I am fortunate to have woken up. I am alive, I have a precious human life. I am not going to waste it."
                                                    —The Dalai Lama

Gratitude is heaven itself.

                                                    —William Blake

Rejoice Always

James Martin, SJ

Here's a shocking thing that I learned during theology studies, specifically during our preaching class. "From time to time," said our professor, "it's okay not to focus on the Gospel when you're preaching on Sundays." What? Really? I thought you had to preach on the *readings*. "Well, yes," he said, "the church's documents on preaching recommend focusing on the readings—but that means not just the Gospel, but also the first and second readings; the psalms; or even the prayers of the Mass."

Today is a good time to exercise that freedom, because the second reading fits perfectly with Gaudete Sunday. The term, by the way, comes from the first words of the opening antiphon of the Mass, "Rejoice in the Lord always," which, oddly, we don't say. And the Latin for "rejoice" is *Gaudete.*

But that term may seem out of place if we look only at the Gospel, where John talks about the One who is to come: it sounds hopeful, but not really that *joyful.* John is approached by some priests and Levites who seem interested, curious, wondering, even hopeful about who he is. The Hebrew Scriptures had predicted the return of Elijah, so maybe this was him. But John makes clear he is only a voice in the wilderness, not fit even to do what a slave would do for the coming Messiah. So, as I said, hopeful, but not particularly joyful in tone.

It is today's second reading that fits the theme of joy much more closely. But it also may be somewhat baffling. Because at the beginning of the reading a strange little phrase upends the typical conception of St. Paul as a cranky, grumpy prude. Paul says, "Rejoice always." And, as we heard, he also says this in the opening antiphon from Philippians, "Rejoice in the Lord always!"

But how in God's name, literally, are we supposed to rejoice always? Does that mean that we're bad Christians if we're not always happy? Well, let's look at that passage a little more carefully.

By common consent, First Thessalonians is the earliest of Paul's letters and, therefore, the earliest writing in the entire New Testament. It was most likely written in Athens or Corinth around A.D. 50. As such, it *predates* the four Gospels and the Acts of the Apostles. Here, Paul is writing to the Christian community that he had founded in Thessalonica, located in the Roman province of Macedonia, on the northern shore of the Aegean Sea. In his brief letter, he encourages his fellow believers to have confidence in the second coming of Jesus, which they thought would happen within their lifetime.

Unlike some of Paul's other letters, he's not responding to any heated theological debate raging within the Christian community in the region. Nor is he scolding his fellow Christians for some litany of horrible sins. Instead, he is mainly encouraging them to lead holy lives. The beginning of the letter, in fact, contains generous praise of the conduct of the Christians in Thessalonica, who he says are an example to other churches in the region. So it's a very gentle letter.

Now back to that remarkable phrase, which is part of a triad of Christian practices: "Rejoice always, pray without ceasing, give thanks in all circumstances; for this is the will of God in Christ Jesus for you."

You could spend a lifetime meditating on that one sentence. You could spend a lifetime meditating on just the words "rejoice always." But is it possible?

Realistically, what does it mean to "rejoice always"? Well, first of all, it doesn't mean that you cannot be sad about suffering or that you have to ignore the tragedies in the world around you. But at first blush, Paul's words certainly seem to imply this to be the case. I mean, we encounter sadness in our lives and we see sadness in other lives, as well as great injustice. Think of all the sick people we know, or the great economic disparities in the world. How can we be "rejoicing"?

Well, Thessalonica in the time of St. Paul was hardly a paradise. Under the heel of Imperial Rome, many in the town were living as slaves. Those who were free may have been poor, illiterate and unable to obtain what we would consider even basic medical care. The Thessalonians would have fully understood the meaning of suffering. And the Christians among them would have known persecution, something that Paul alludes to in the first few lines of his letter. Paul knew about suffering, too. So how could Paul ask them to turn a blind eye to the realities of life?

He wasn't. St. Paul was pointing to something

deeper. It is easy to be joyful when you are happy. Or to be joyful during those fleeting moments when the world seems like a fair and just place for everyone. But how can you be joyful in sad times, and in the face of injustice? You can be joyful because joy is deeper than happiness and is not about a thing or an object, but about something else: God. Joy is happiness in God.

One of the most vivid memories I have as a Jesuit novice was being invited to a predominantly African American church in Boston. Before this, I had never been in such a church. Yet, from the moment the choir began singing the entrance hymn, an African-American spiritual, I felt swept away into a chorus of joy. Years later, during my time working in Eastern Africa, I would experience that same ebullience in the songs of the churches in the Nairobi slums, where Kenyans would be packed shoulder to shoulder as they shouted out the words of Swahili hymns. What these two groups had in common was not simply the color of their skin, but their abiding confidence in God.

Joy, deeper than happiness, is a virtue that finds its foundation in the knowledge that we are loved by God. For Christians, the knowledge that Jesus has been raised from the dead is a constant cause for joy, even in tough times. This does not mean that suffering does not bring sadness. Of course it does. But suffering is not the last word—in Jesus's life, or in ours. And that knowledge can lead us to a deeper joy. Even in the midst of difficulties.

Sadness is an appropriate and natural response to suffering. And God desires that we be honest about our sadness, and share it in prayer with God. The knowledge that God is with us, however, and that God accompanies us, can lead us to a confident joy that can carry us through difficult, and sometimes unbearable, times.

Likewise, the passage "rejoice always" does not mean that we should simply "look on the bright side" in the face of injustice. The anger that rises within you over an unjust situation is a sign that God is moving you to address that injustice. God speaks to you through your anger at what you see, through your disgust over what you have read, or your shock over what someone has told you. How else would God move you to action? This is particularly the case when it is an injustice visited upon another person, since anger over an injustice to yourself (rightful though the anger may be) may be tinged with selfishness and a sense of wounded pride.

"Let's say you passed a homeless person sitting beside a fancy restaurant; diners come out, after having spent hundreds of dollars on their meal, but fail to give the person even a glance, let alone a few dollars or a kind word." You might be angry or sad. You would probably be moved to give to that person some of your own money, and maybe even spend some time with him. But you certainly wouldn't say to yourself, much less to him, "Be happy!" Witnessing the injustice, you would try, as far as you could, to lessen it. Out of such strong emotions and holy anger are born great works of charity.

Where is the joy, then? It comes from a loving trust in God, in the awareness that God is working through the compassion you feel, in the knowledge that God desires a just world where the poor are treated fairly, and in the trust that God will help those who heed His voice to help bring about justice. So, there is joy.

Of course, this is what John the Baptist is talking about in the Gospel today. "Make straight the way of the Lord" means not physically leveling a path that Jesus can walk on; but bringing justice into the world, making things "right" with God; preparing a just world, and repenting of greed. So his message is not just a hopeful one, but a joyful one, as well.

But, let's go back to St. Paul. One important key to his suggestion is that all three parts of his triad of Christian practices are bound together. Rejoice always. Pray without ceasing. In all circumstances, give thanks. So: joy, prayer and gratitude—they're all connected.

Joy, for example, springs from gratitude. When we recall things, events or people for which and for whom we are grateful, our joy increases. Prayer also supports the other two virtues. A contemplative awareness of the world and an attitude of prayerful attentiveness make it easier to see life's blessings. Finally, joy moves us to gratitude.

Likewise, our gratitude over good news can lead to joy. Joy can also move us to prayer. In our joy we want to be with God, to share our joyful life, gratefully, in prayer—just as we would share joy with a friend. Thus, each virtue supports the others in a complex spiritual interplay. Prayer awakens gratitude. Gratitude leads to joy. And joy moves us to prayer. In this way, we are able to follow Paul's gentle advice to the Thessalonians from almost 2,000 years ago.

Many modern believers think of St. Paul not as the Apostle of Joy, but as the Apostle of Gloom. He is usually characterized solely as a stern moralizer, intent on frustrating authentic human emotions, obsessed with tamping down human sexuality. Yet, here in his earliest letter, Paul is recommending something positive.

There were other Christian communities that needed to hear sterner words. But to the Christians of Thessalonica and to Christians today, the Apostle Paul advises three things. The first of these is joy.

So on this Gaudete Sunday, I say to you, St. Paul says to you, the church says to you, and Jesus Christ says to you: "Rejoice always!"

5

Gloria

Denise Levertov

Praise the wet snow
falling early.
Praise the shadow
my neighbor's chimney casts on the tile roof
even this gray October day that should, they say,
have been golden.
   Praise
the invisible sun burning beyond
the white cold sky, giving us
light and the chimney's shadow.
Praise
god or the gods, the unknown,
that which imagined us, which stays
our hand,

our murderous hand,

                      and gives us
still,
in the shadow of death,
          our daily life,
          and the dream still
of goodwill, of peace on earth.
Praise
flow and change, night and
the pulse of day.

6

The Beauty and Promise of Christian Gratitude

Patrick Manning

Thanksgiving is a wonderful holiday. This week families and friends across the country will gather together to celebrate the occasion by converging upon a single crowded household. Tables will be elegantly set and the turkeys will be roasted (and more than a few burnt). It offers all the things that make holidays enjoyable (time away from work, good food, and good company) with fewer of the things that make other holidays so stressful (like Christmas gift shopping).

Still, there are some less savory aspects about the way we observe Thanksgiving. It is at the very least ironic and perhaps even spiritually counterproductive that, on a day purportedly devoted to expressing gratitude for all that we have been given, for many of us our attention is devoted primarily to the anticipation of the Thanksgiving meal and to feeding our appetites for watching NFL games and shopping for Black Friday bargains, which have become our other essential rituals of the day.

Now there is nothing inherently wrong with shopping or watching a football game. Nor is it necessarily a mark of moral depravity to indulge in the occasional feast. To the contrary, Scripture repeatedly likens God's reign to a great banquet and a wedding feast. The problem is that modern mass marketing and consumer culture do more to multiply people's desires than they do to foster gratitude. In truth, if we examine the matter more closely, we see that the problem runs deeper: the regrettable aspects of our contemporary Thanksgiving celebrations are only the latest manifestations of that perennial struggle within the human heart, the struggle between worldly concern and transcendent calling.

Always Hungry, Always Searching

The primary source of tension derives from our creaturely constitution. We human beings are hardwired to persistently seek the satisfaction of our needs. We hunger when our bodies need nourishment, thirst when they need hydration, and lust because it is necessary for the propagation of our species. These desires are strong, and they are strong for a reason: if we were to neglect the functions to which these desires drive us, we would not survive. In this sense, these desires serve an important purpose in the world God created, namely, sustaining life. Yet this is not all there is to human life. Although we share these primal desires in common with simpler animals, humans also experience desires that are not strictly necessary for our survival: we desire to be loved, esteemed and to be spiritually fulfilled. Our spiritual yearnings demand satisfaction not merely for us to survive, but to live a truly meaningful life. These transcendent yearnings represent the second source of tension in our lives.

So it is that, on account of both biological and spiritual drives, we are strongly disposed to focus our attention on what we lack. This reality of human existence finds apt expression in the Passenger song "Let Her Go," which was a mainstay on the radio earlier this year. The refrain of the song reads:

But you only need the light when it's burning low,
Only miss the sun when it starts to snow,
Only know you love her when you let her go,
Only know you've been high when you're feeling low,

Only hate the road when you're missin' home,
Only know you love her when you let her go.

The theme of human desiring and concern has garnered considerable attention not only among artists but also among many notable philosophers and theologians. For example, the great 20th-century philosopher Martin Heidegger describes concern (*Sorge* in German) as constitutive of our very manner of existence. "Being-in-the-world," Heidegger writes, "is essentially concern."

Becoming aware of the way concern constrains our attention and orients our lives is a crucial step on the path to self-knowledge. When we grow in this awareness, it illuminates a myriad of phenomena in our lives: It helps us to understand why that person at work complains about everything. It explains why the first two seasons of "House of Cards," when the Underwoods were still aspiring to the White House, were more riveting than the third in which they had achieved their aim. It explains how we can turn a holiday founded as an occasion for giving thanks for what we have into a day of desiring and indulging in far more than we need. It helps us to understand (as well as anything can) why human beings, whom God had given everything they needed to be happy, would grasp at the one thing forbidden to them.

Periodically across the centuries, "enlightened" thinkers and religious leaders have decried human desiring as the source of our suffering and called for its eradication, whether by the disciplined use of reason or by ascetic measures. However, all such efforts to eliminate human desire have and always will prove futile. There is simply no end to our desiring in this life. As soon as one concern fades away, another crops up in its place—concern for social acceptance, for good grades, for reciprocation of romantic feelings, for professional status, for an estranged family member, for bills that need to be paid, for the success of a party or fundraiser, for sexual fulfillment, for a child's well-being, for one's declining health. Many of us live much of our lives under the illusion that, if we could only obtain this salary level or the affection of that person, we would be content. However, it is an illusion indeed. St. Augustine summed up the matter well in his famous profession, "our hearts are restless until they rest in [God]." In other words, there is no satisfying the human heart this side of heaven.

If we are to find any measure of lasting peace in this lifetime, we have to abandon the fool's errand of satisfying here and now every desire that sets upon us. This is not to say that we must abandon hope of eventually fulfilling our hearts' deepest desire. Implied in Augustine's famous words is the belief that our desires do ultimately find fulfillment in God and that the insatiability of our worldly desires leads us to God. We are never satisfied in this world because we are created for more than this world can give. If this is true, it would be a double folly to attempt to eliminate our desires—in the first case because such efforts are futile and in the second because our desires may actually be leading us to God.

Naming Our Gifts

So if we cannot satisfy all our desires and we cannot eliminate them, how are we to deal with this desiring within us that at once orients us to God and yet threatens to lead us astray? According to the inherited wisdom of the Christian tradition, the most reliable path lies, not in feeding or repressing our desires, but rather in rightly ordering them. In this endeavor gratitude is a powerful agent. Each of us has experienced at some point the power of gratitude to put things back in perspective and to restore our awareness of things we had taken for granted. Who has not felt gratitude for a warm home when returning from the cold, inclement outdoors or for a cool glass of water after an exhausting workout? Our gratitude reaches new heights in those times when we are helpless to obtain what we need. One need only think of a parent whose deathly ill child has received a life-saving organ transplant. In all such cases, the alleviation of a particularly poignant need restores our appreciation for gifts that we tend to overlook on account of their fixity in our lives.

I believe that experiences like these provide us with a clue as to why, throughout the course of salvation history, God has repeatedly encouraged God's people to form habits and rituals of gratitude. Look at the ancient Israelites. If ever a group of people had reason to be grateful, it was they. Time and again they found themselves on the brink of destruction—as slaves in Egypt, dying of thirst in the desert, hemmed in by enemies in the promised land, carried off into exile—only to be rescued by God in every instance. Their reasons to be grateful were many, and yet over and over their desires for pleasure, glory and security caused them to stray from the one true Source of peace and joy. Therefore, whenever it proved necessary to refocus the Israelites' desires and renew their fidelity, God persistently reminded them of all the good God had done for them in the past: "Remember these things, O Jacob, and Israel . . . " (Isa 44:21). Following this cue, the people of Israel marked out special holy days of thanksgiving and incorporated prayers of gratitude and remembrance into their daily routines. To this day these occasions for giving thanks serve as reminders of God's goodness and opportunities for turning back to God.

Our situation as contemporary Christians is no different . . . or at least it would be no different were it not for God's intervention in the person of Jesus Christ. Like the people of Israel, we live in constant threat of destruction—if not the death of the body, then certainly the death of the soul wrought by sin. As was the case with Israel, God has come to our aid time and again, most definitively in the incarnation, death, and resurrection of Jesus. Like the people of Israel, we easily forget what God has done for us whenever a friendship becomes strained or finances get tight. For this reason, we need to be constantly reminded of God's saving work lest we become consumed by our concerns and desires.

Recognizing this need, before Jesus entered into his Paschal Mystery that would deliver us from the power of sin and death, he gathered his disciples around him and, breaking the bread and sharing the cup, commanded them, "Do this in remembrance of me" (Lk 22:19). Giving them his body and blood in this way, Jesus united his self-donation on the cross to common bread and wine, which symbolize for us life and happiness. In so doing, Jesus provided us with the concrete, sacramental means of centering our lives in gratitude and thanksgiving for the salvation God has achieved for us.

Looking at the Eucharist—a word that means "thanksgiving"—in this light helps us to understand why the church has proclaimed it the "source and summit of the Christian life" (*Cathechism of the Catholic Church*, No. 1324). Because we are neurologically disposed to focus on what we lack and because every day and week brings with it new worries and preoccupations, achieving peace and perspective in our lives requires intentional effort to counter our desires with remembrances of the specific hopes and needs that God has already met. Because our thoughts and feelings are greatly influenced by our habits and physical condition, we need a fixture in our routine to help us remember and dwell in enjoyment of the many blessings in our lives. The Eucharist is this fixture.

Here in the United States we devote one day of

the year to giving thanks. That is well and good, but it is far from adequate. Life's concerns rush in upon us on a daily basis. If we are to keep from being overwhelmed by those concerns, we need to center our lives in gratitude on a weekly if not a daily basis. Countless Christians have discovered for themselves the calming, centering power of the Eucharist. By remembering what God has done for us and joining in Jesus' sacrifice of thanks, we find a momentary rest for our souls and a means of reordering our desires toward God, their true source and goal.

I offer the above as food for thought as we prepare for the approaching Thanksgiving holiday. On November 26 we do well to gather with family and celebrate life's blessings with a hearty meal. However, rather than building anticipation for one day of overeating, we would do better to build anticipation for the banquet of love that God has prepared for us in the next life and that we foretaste here and now in the Eucharist. For in this sacramental meal—and even more so in the heavenly feast it symbolizes—we encounter that which alone can satisfy, not our stomachs', but our hearts' deepest desire.

Thank Yous

This is a wonderful day. I've never seen this one before.

—Maya Angelou

Joy is what happens to us when we allow ourselves to recognize how good things really are.

—Marianne Williamson

It's enough for me to be sure that you and I exist at this moment.

—Gabriel García Márquez

Meditation on Gratitude and Joy

Jack Kornfield

*If we cannot be happy in spite of our difficulties,
what good is our spiritual practice?*
—Maha Ghosananda

Buddhist monks begin each day with a chant of gratitude for the blessings of their life. Native American elders begin each ceremony with grateful prayers to mother earth and father sky, to the four directions, to the animal, plant, and mineral brothers and sisters who share our earth and support our life. In Tibet, the monks and nuns even offer prayers of gratitude for the suffering they have been given: "Grant that I might have enough suffering to awaken in the deepest possible compassion and wisdom."

The aim of spiritual life is to awaken a joyful freedom, a benevolent and compassionate heart in spite of everything.

Gratitude is a gracious acknowledgment of all that sustains us, a bow to our blessings, great and small, an appreciation of the moments of good fortune that sustain our life every day. We have so much to be grateful for.

Gratitude is confidence in life itself. It is not sentimental, not jealous, nor judgmental. Gratitude does not envy or compare. Gratitude receives in wonder the myriad offerings of the rain and the earth, the care that supports every single life.

As gratitude grows it gives rise to joy. We experience the courage to rejoice in our own good fortune and in the good fortune of others.

Joy is natural to an open heart. In it, we are not afraid of pleasure. We do not mistakenly believe it is disloyal to the suffering of the world to honor the happiness we have been given.

Like gratitude, joy gladdens the heart. We can be joyful for people we love, for moments of goodness, for sunlight and trees, and for the breath within our breast. And as our joy grows we finally discover a happiness without cause. Like an innocent child who does not have to do anything to be happy, we can rejoice in life itself, in being alive.

Let yourself sit quietly and at ease. Allow your body to be relaxed and open, your breath natural, your heart easy. Begin the practice of gratitude by feeling how year after year you have cared for your own life. Now let yourself begin to acknowledge all that has supported you in this care:

With gratitude I remember the people, animals,
plants, insects, creatures of the sky and sea,
air and water, fire and earth, all whose joyful
exertion blesses my life every day.

With gratitude I remember the care and labor of a
thousand generations of elders and ancestors
who came before me.

I offer my gratitude for the safety and well-being I
have been given.

I offer my gratitude for the blessing of this earth I
have been given.

I offer my gratitude for the measure of health I have
been given.

I offer my gratitude for the family and friends I
have been given.

I offer my gratitude for the community I have been
given.

*I offer my gratitude for the teachings and lessons I
have been given.*

I offer my gratitude for the life I have been given.

Just as we are grateful for our blessings, so we can
be grateful for the blessings of others.

Continue to breathe gently. Bring to mind someone you care about, someone it is easy to rejoice
for. Picture them and feel the natural joy you have
for their well-being, for their happiness and success.
With each breath, offer them your grateful, heartfelt
wishes:

May you be joyful.

May your happiness increase.

May you not be separated from great happiness.

*May your good fortune and the causes for your joy
and happiness increase.*

Sense the sympathetic joy and caring in each phrase.
When you feel some degree of natural gratitude for
the happiness of this loved one, extend this practice to
another person you care about. Recite the same simple
phrases that express your heart's intention.

Then gradually open the meditation to include
neutral people, difficult people, and even enemies—
until you extend sympathetic joy to all beings everywhere, young and old, near and far.

The Color of Gratitude

Robert Morneau

My choice is purple,
recalling the clover in a boyhood meadow.
Deo Gratias!
Others might choose red,
watching the fireball sun sink into the ocean.
Deo Gratias!
Still others opt for blue,
robin-egg blue telling of hidden life.
Deo Gratias!

Gratitude is a rainbow
sun and rain shining in the same room.
Gratitude is a peanut-butter sandwich (toasted),
knowing that it is enough,
Gratitude is to dwell in mystery,
the enigma of being loved,
of just being.

All Is Grace

Henri Nouwen

"We are really grateful for all the good things. . . .
We simply have to accept or try to forget the painful moments." The attitude expressed in these words
made me aware of how often we tend to divide our
past into good things to remember with gratitude
and painful things to accept or forget. Once we accept this division, however, we quickly develop a
mentality in which we hope to collect more good
memories than bad memories, more things to be
grateful for than things to be resentful about, more
things to celebrate than things to complain about.
But this way of thinking, which at first glance seems
quite natural, prevents us from truly allowing our
whole past to be the source from which we live our
future. Is this the gratitude to which the Gospel
calls us?

Gratitude is not a simple emotion or an obvious attitude. It is a difficult discipline to constantly reclaim my whole past as the concrete way in which God has led me to this moment and is sending me into the future. It is hard precisely because it challenges me to face the painful moments—experiences of rejection and abandonment, feelings of loss and failure—and gradually to discover in them the pruning hands of God purifying my heart for deeper love, stronger hope, and broader faith. Jesus says to his disciples that although they are as intimately related to him as branches are to the vine, they still need to be pruned in order to bear more fruit (John 15:1–5). Pruning means cutting, reshaping, removing what diminishes vitality. . . .

Grateful people are those who can celebrate even the pains of life because they trust that when harvest time comes the fruit will show that the pruning was not punishment but purification.

I am gradually learning that the call to gratitude asks us to say "everything is grace." When our gratitude for the past is only partial, our hope for a new future can never be full. . . . If we are to be truly ready for a new task in the service of God, truly joyful at the prospect of a new vocation, truly free to be sent into a new mission, our entire past, gathered into the spaciousness of a converted heart, must become the source of energy that moves us toward the future.

Love and Gratitude

Mother Mary Joseph Rogers, MM

We find the motive for such a life as ours expressed in the beautiful prayer of love and gratitude:

> *"God, I love you not simply to be saved. I love you because you are my God."*

How lovely such gratitude! Gratitude is a rare virtue and one which most surely should be ours because so much has been and is given to us. We should express our gratitude for all favors. Christ knew the proportion of grateful hearts. Cultivate the virtue of gratitude for supernatural reasons.

We get everything because we are the servants of God—not of ourselves!

Stand Up and Go; Your Faith Has Saved You

Joel Blunk

Giving thanks is central to Luke's story of the ten lepers. When they realized they were healed, only one of them began to shout praises to God. He turned back, fell at Jesus' feet and thanked him, expressing gratitude for the healing he received.

We're not sure about the other nine. Perhaps they were too busy celebrating, too eager to get on with their lives, or maybe they simply lacked the faith to see the true significance of what had happened and how it had happened. But one had to go back and pay his respects. He recognized he'd been given a gift and that Jesus had done something remarkable for him. Through his actions, the leper reveals a humble spirit and demonstrates a rare sensitivity to the grace of God.

Key to the story is the realization that something more than mere healing had taken place. The leper was made well (v. 19). What Jesus did was to not stop with the curing of the man's leprosy; he provided care for the whole of who the man was.

The Greek verb *sozo* meaning "to be made well" is used here in the original text. Another translation for that verb is "saved." Salvation, as it is intended, is God's provision for the whole of who we are. Through Jesus, God touched every aspect of this man's life and made it new in every way. He experienced complete transformation through the saving grace of God's love.

God touches our lives too. And God offers us transformation—a healing wellness that reaches deep to our very core. It changes us, frees us, enabling us to be more completely whom God created us to be. Like the leper who was suddenly free to run, shout, and express himself genuinely and authentically, we should so too relish this opportunity.

Several years ago I was granted a sabbatical that took my family and me to West Africa, where we lived for several weeks in a rural village in the country of Togo. Though we didn't speak the native language and our French was limited, "Thank you" was easily understood. Regularly when we'd express our thanks for food offered, shelter provided, or the hospitality our African neighbors were so generous to provide, the response we'd get was, "Thanks be to God!" Or, to put it in the vernacular, "Don't thank me, God is the reason for this!" Their faith in God was strong, and though they had very little by U.S. standards, they knew that all they had was a gift from God.

I wonder why I'm so slow to make the connection myself. It's something the one leper in Luke's story picked up on right away and responded to with great enthusiasm. The more I reflect the more I fear I'm more like the other nine, and I'm probably exaggerating to say I notice one tenth of the time!

So what about those other nine? Certainly they knew their skin was healed, but did they know it was an act of God? Did they know that what was being offered was more than physical healing? Did they have any clue of the complete wellness and salvation being handed to them?

Apparently, only one saw this salvation for what it was in full, and only one received the gift with gratitude and thanksgiving.

For the gift of God's love given for us, we too have the opportunity to show our appreciation. Thankfulness is a natural response. As Meister Eckhart said, "If in your lifetime the only prayer you offer is thanks, that would suffice." To show appreciation for God and to God is always an appropriate response.

In this way, the leper models faith for us. He goes back to say, "Thank you, God, for what you've done for me." His action helps us to see that gratitude is a key component of faith. His gratitude is shown not to celebrate his own faith, but to show his appreciation for the faith God in Christ has in him! In the end, his gesture is an act of faith itself.

Gratitude is a natural reaction to what God has done and is doing in our lives. But it is not just the words we say. As powerful as the words "thank you" can be, our actions always speak louder. Therefore our prayer of thanks should include the way we live our lives. The leper went back, threw himself down at Jesus' feet in an act of reverence and devotion.

What a surprising thing for him to do! And it's made even more surprising when you consider that he was a Samaritan. Samaritans were outsiders, ritually unclean, the enemy, foreigners who were at odds with the Jewish community. Under normal circumstances, the two didn't get along or even speak to each other. And so, this Samaritan is an unlikely model of faith.

Though an outsider and a stranger to Jewish ritual and practice, he was still able to have faith and act on it. In fact, his ability to do so tells us something important about faith: Faith shouldn't be narrowly defined as a set of beliefs or religious practices. It's not correct dogma or right ritual that defines faith in this context, but relationship!

The Samaritan, by way of his turning to Jesus, enters into relationship with him. He draws near, prostrates himself and thanks the new-found Lord of his life. He connects with God through him and relates in response to Jesus' helping hand.

Faith, as revealed through this one, isn't about believing the right thing or professing the right creed, but about complete devotion and commitment to the relationship. Such is at the heart of the great commandment to love one another. Which is why Jesus sent him on his way. Love isn't meant to be insular or narrow, but rather outward and like the universe, ever expanding. So Jesus sent him on his way to love and to serve.

The Samaritan in our text for today got it right. He accepted what was offered and responded with thanks. He drew near to God in praise and thanksgiving, and he went forth a changed man to live a new life of gratitude devoted to God and others. It's likely many came to know God through him. And that's what it's really all about, isn't it? Others knowing the same love we do? Living in gratitude for who God is and for what God is doing in our lives.

The question for us today is, will we do the same? Will we respond in kind? Will we live our lives as if our relationship with God matters? Will our lives reflect the same fidelity and devotion as the tenth leper? Will we express our gratitude completely? Maybe, just maybe, Jesus' words to the tenth leper are for us as well. "Get up and go on your way. Your faith—your relationship with me—has made you well."

Now that's something to be thankful for! Amen.

Thank Yous

We receive this food in gratitude to all beings
Who have helped to bring it to our table,
And vow to respond in turn to those in need
With wisdom and compassion.
                              —Buddhist Blessing

You say grace before meals. All right. But I say
grace before the concert and the opera, and grace
before the play and pantomime, and grace before
I open a book, and grace before sketching, painting,
swimming, fencing, boxing, walking, playing,
dancing and grace before I dip the pen in the ink.
                              —G.K. Chesterton

Thank you, God, for this good life and forgive us if
we do not love it enough.
                              —Garrison Keillor

12

My Own Life

Oliver Sacks

A month ago, I felt that I was in good health, even robust health. At 81, I still swim a mile a day. But my luck has run out—a few weeks ago I learned that I have multiple metastases in the liver. Nine years ago it was discovered that I had a rare tumor of the eye, an ocular melanoma. The radiation and lasering to remove the tumor ultimately left me blind in that eye. But though ocular melanomas metastasize in perhaps 50 percent of cases, given the particulars of my own case, the likelihood was much smaller. I am among the unlucky ones.

I feel grateful that I have been granted nine years of good health and productivity since the original diagnosis, but now I am face to face with dying. The cancer occupies a third of my liver, and though its advance may be slowed, this particular sort of cancer cannot be halted.

It is up to me now to choose how to live out the months that remain to me. I have to live in the richest, deepest, most productive way I can. In this I am encouraged by the words of one of my favorite philosophers, David Hume, who, upon learning that he was mortally ill at age 65, wrote a short autobiography in a single day in April of 1776. He titled it "My Own Life."

"I now reckon upon a speedy dissolution," he wrote. "I have suffered very little pain from my disorder; and what is more strange, have, notwithstanding the great decline of my person, never suffered a moment's abatement of my spirits. I possess the same ardour as ever in study, and the same gaiety in company."

I have been lucky enough to live past 80, and the 15 years allotted to me beyond Hume's three score and five have been equally rich in work and love. In that time, I have published five books and completed an autobiography (rather longer than Hume's few pages) to be published this spring; I have several other books nearly finished.

Hume continued, "I am . . . a man of mild dispositions, of command of temper, of an open, social, and cheerful humor, capable of attachment, but little susceptible of enmity, and of great moderation in all my passions."

Here I depart from Hume. While I have enjoyed loving relationships and friendships and have no real enmities, I cannot say (nor would anyone who knows me say) that I am a man of mild dispositions. On the contrary, I am a man of vehement disposition, with violent enthusiasms, and extreme immoderation in all my passions.

And yet, one line from Hume's essay strikes me as especially true: "It is difficult," he wrote, "to be more detached from life than I am at present."

Over the last few days, I have been able to see my life as from a great altitude, as a sort of landscape, and with a deepening sense of the connection of all its parts. This does not mean I am finished with life.

On the contrary, I feel intensely alive, and I want and hope in the time that remains to deepen my friendships, to say farewell to those I love, to write more, to travel if I have the strength, to achieve new levels of understanding and insight.

This will involve audacity, clarity and plain speaking; trying to straighten my accounts with the world. But there will be time, too, for some fun (and even some silliness, as well).

I feel a sudden clear focus and perspective. There is

no time for anything inessential. I must focus on myself, my work and my friends. I shall no longer look at "NewsHour" every night. I shall no longer pay any attention to politics or arguments about global warming.

This is not indifference but detachment—I still care deeply about the Middle East, about global warming, about growing inequality, but these are no longer my business; they belong to the future. I rejoice when I meet gifted young people—even the one who biopsied and diagnosed my metastases. I feel the future is in good hands.

I have been increasingly conscious, for the last ten years or so, of deaths among my contemporaries. My generation is on the way out, and each death I have felt as an abruption, a tearing away of part of myself. There will be no one like us when we are gone, but then there is no one like anyone else, ever. When people die, they cannot be replaced. They leave holes that cannot be filled, for it is the fate—the genetic and neural fate—of every human being to be a unique individual, to find his own path, to live his own life, to die his own death.

I cannot pretend I am without fear. But my predominant feeling is one of gratitude. I have loved and been loved; I have been given much and I have given something in return; I have read and traveled and thought and written. I have had an intercourse with the world, the special intercourse of writers and readers.

Above all, I have been a sentient being, a thinking animal, on this beautiful planet, and that in itself has been an enormous privilege and adventure.

13

For Your Goodness—A Prayer of Gratitude in Trying Times

Brendan Busse, SJ

Few moments are as wonderful as when you come to know the goodness of a thing. Not your liking it, needing it, wanting it, or not. But rather, the moment you come to recognize its fundamental goodness and come to accept that its goodness is enough.

When this happens you forget yourself and you fall in love with the object of your attention as you adopt a reverent posture of wonder before it. You express only gratitude for having noticed it. You desire only to place yourself in its service, to share, in some small way, in the grace of its presence. It could be anything really, or anyone, because when we recognize goodness, when we are free enough to recognize it, we are actually reverencing God.

But we're not always keen on goodness. Sometimes we fail to recognize it. Or sometimes it's not enough for us. When the simple goodness of a thing being what it is isn't enough for us we begin to do terrible things. We make ourselves cruel judges of that which the Creator thought worthy of creation. We make our petty desires the measuring stick of a reality whose complexity far exceeds our understanding. And, at our very worst, we place our fear between us and the heart of things, we reel back and pull the trigger. We kill the one who came to save us.

Few moments are as terrible as when we fail to recognize the goodness of a thing. Few moments are as devastating as when we deny the gift of our goodness and refuse to accept that we belong to each other. We seem to be living through one of those moments now. It seems very difficult these days to recognize our goodness.

❖ ❖ ❖

I once lived with a Jesuit who had a peculiar pronunciation of the word *goodness*. He was learning English and struggled with the double-o in *good*, such that *goodness* always came out sounding like *God-ness*. His pronunciation was off, but his usage was perfect. Like many language learners who find a reliable phrase in their foreign tongue, he used it a lot. Someone would make a bad joke—*Oh my God-ness!* Someone would reveal a special dessert—*Oh my God-ness!* Someone would ask him about his studies—*Oh my God-ness!*

His odd pronunciation caught my attention, but his total sincerity became a revelation. He taught me something of what we might mean by that expression, that we are as reverent as we are surprised, and that, sometimes, our wonder is enough. Perhaps a love that recognizes goodness, without adding conditions or judgments, perhaps that is the kind of love we all need. Perhaps accepting the self-giving goodness of things is enough. Perhaps.

❖ ❖ ❖

Our recognition of goodness is always our coming into the presence of God. This is the wisdom of worship, the righteousness of reverence, the mystery of revelation. This is the great gift of self-giving love, the peaceful beauty of things merely being what they are. But this grace of recognition also helps us to know when things aren't yet as they ought to be. The present of goodness is also goodness becoming.

There is goodness in suffering love, in righteous anger, in witnessing unto death. There is goodness in the struggle for justice, the tenderness of mercy, the surrender of sacrifice. There is goodness in the reality of truth, even and especially when that truth is difficult or dangerous to speak. There is goodness in each of these precisely because they are instances of our witness to the beauty of life and our insistence on the depravity of its enemies. And so too, in times of terror, we cry out—*Oh my goodness! Oh my God!*

❖ ❖ ❖

The goodness of a thing is not an abstract idea, but something to be experienced. This is important, however difficult, to remember in times of violence and confusion, division and despair, even death. We will not think our way to goodness. We will only come to know the goodness of a difficult moment by our living through it. If we want for the grace of knowing God in all things we must also want for the courage to do the will of God in every moment.

Spanish has a great word for this—*la bondad*—which can mean both goodness and kindness. We generally think of kindness as something to do and goodness as something to be. The truth, of course, is both. Our goodness is made known in kindness. And kindness is an expression of our kinship—the goodness of our being of one flesh, our being bound together, our belonging to each other. Our kindness is our share in the God-ness of things.

❖❖❖

A striking image surfaced after a sniper opened fire on a crowd in Dallas, a dramatic photo of a group of people surrounding a baby carriage as the shooting began. These people, apparently strangers to one another, placed their bodies between the bullets and the baby. Seeing this image moved me first to tears and then to prayer.

Few moments are as wonderful as when you come to know the goodness of a thing.

I give thanks for all of those who have ever felt the cold steel of fear pressed against their hearts and yet didn't fail to recognize the goodness of life, didn't fail to risk themselves for the sake of that goodness. It is so very good to see you. Your life matters absolutely to mine. I want nothing more than to be with you, to praise you, and to thank you, for your goodness.

14

The Sun of Awareness

Thich Nhat Hanh

One evening I returned to my hermitage from a walk in the hills, and I found that all the doors and windows of the hermitage had been blown open. When I left the house, I hadn't secured them, and a cold wind blew through the house, opened the windows, and scattered the papers from the desk all over the room. Immediately I closed the doors and windows, lit a lamp, picked up the papers, and arranged them neatly on my desk. Then I started a fire in the fireplace, and soon the crackling logs brought warmth back to the room.

Sometimes in a crowd we feel tired, cold, and lonely. We may wish to withdraw to be by ourselves and become warm again, as I did at the hermitage sitting by the fire, protected from the cold, damp wind.

Our senses are our windows to the outside world, and sometimes the wind blows and disturbs everything within us. Many of us leave our windows open all the time, allowing the sights and sounds of the world to invade us, penetrate us, and expose our sad, troubled selves. We feel so cold and lonely and afraid. Do you ever find yourself watching an awful TV program, unable to turn it off? The raucous noises, explosions of gunfire, are upsetting. Yet you don't get up and turn it off. Why do you torture yourself in this way? Don't you want to close your windows? Are you afraid of solitude—the emptiness and the loneliness you may find when you face yourself alone?

We are what we feel and perceive. If we are angry, we are the anger. If we are in love, we are the love. If we look at a snowy mountain peak, we are the mountain. Watching a bad TV program, we are the TV program. While dreaming, we are the dream. We can be anything we want, even without a magic wand. So why do we open our windows to bad movies and TV programs, movies made by sensationalist producers in search of easy money, movies which make our hearts pound, our fists tighten, and send us back into the streets exhausted? Who allows such movies and TV programs to be made? Especially for the very young. We do! We are too undemanding, too ready to watch whatever is on the screen, too lonely, lazy, or bored to create our own lives. We turn on the TV and leave it on, allowing someone else to guide us, shape us, and destroy us. Losing ourselves in this way is leaving our fate in the hands of others who may not be acting responsibly. We must be aware of what kinds of programs do harm to our nervous systems, our minds, and our hearts, and which programs and films benefit us.

I am not just talking about movies and TV programs. All around us, how many lures are set there by our fellows and ourselves? In a single day, how many times do we become lost and scattered because of them? We must be very careful to protect our fate and our peace. That does not mean shutting all our windows, for there are many miracles in the world we call "outside." Open your windows to these miracles. Look at any one of them with the light of awareness. Even while sitting beside a clear, flowing stream listening to beautiful music, or watching an excellent movie, do not entrust yourself entirely to the stream, the music, or the film. Continue to be aware of yourself and your breathing. With the sun of awareness shining in us, we can avoid most dangers—the stream will be purer, the music more harmonious, and the soul of the artist completely visible in the film.

Around us, life bursts forth with miracles—a glass of water, a ray of sunshine, a leaf, a caterpillar, a flower, laughter, raindrops. If you live in awareness, it is easy to see miracles everywhere. Each human being is a multiplicity of miracles. Eyes that see thousands of colors, shapes, and forms; ears that hear a bee flying or a thunderclap; a brain that ponders a speck of dust as easily as the entire cosmos; a heart that beats in rhythm with the heartbeat of all beings. When we are tired and feel discouraged by life's daily struggles, we may not notice these miracles, but they are always there.

Have a look at the apple tree in your yard. Look at it with complete attention. It is truly a miracle. If you notice it, you will take good care of it, and you too are part of its miraculousness. Even after caring for it for only a week, its leaves are already greener and shinier. It is exactly the same with the people who are around you. Under the influence of awareness, you become more attentive, understanding, and loving, and your presence not only nourishes you and makes you lovelier, it enhances them as well. Our entire society can be changed by one person's peaceful presence.

Our minds create everything. The majestic mountain top, brilliant with snow, is you yourself when you contemplate it. Its existence depends on your awareness. When you close your eyes, as long as your mind is present, the mountain is there. Sitting in meditation, with several sense-windows closed, you feel the presence of the whole universe. Why? Because the mind is there. If your eyes are closed, it is so that you can see better. The sights and sounds of the world are not your "enemies." Your "enemy" is forgetfulness, the absence of mindfulness.

15

Fill Me at Daybreak with Gratitude

Joyce Rupp

Satisfy us in the morning with your steadfast love,
so that we may rejoice and be glad all our days.
— PSALM 90:14

Each dawn brings the birth of a new day and an opportunity for entering into sacred communion with the Source of Life. As the darkness of night lifts and the rays of light open up the world to us again, we enter into a brief period of time that holds a distinctive quality of freshness. Each emergence of daylight conveys a miracle worth attending. Every morning offers an opportunity to thank the Creator for our life.

I am a "morning person" who enjoys getting up

early, going for a prayerful walk, returning home and sitting in meditation. This time of day validates my hope. It restores my gratitude for being alive. I have friends who are "night people," preferring to stay up longer and get up later the next day. Can they also pray in the morning? Definitely. Morning prayer begins whenever we arise, not necessarily when the sun comes peeping over the horizon, but most certainly when we coax our bodies out of bed and move from the dark of our sleepiness into the light of restorative energy.

Each of us has to find the best time of day to pray. I truly believe one of the first things required for faithful union with the Holy One, no matter when or how we arise, is to pray some kind of thanksgiving for a new day. Even if we had a restless night that kept us awake with unresolved issues or have been unable to reduce the pain of our bodies, even then the light of a new day invites us to be grateful. Life is simply too precious a gift to assume it will be there for us with the next breath. Existence on planet Earth is simply too wondrous for us to forget the privilege of living upon it.

Morning prayer includes the vital aspect of intentionally uniting ourselves with the One who sustains our life. This prayer may be as simple as standing in quiet gratitude with hands outstretched toward the east, the place of the day's incoming light. How beneficial to renew our trust in the One who breathes in us at that very moment. How easy and right to fill our opened heart with love for all creation in that gesture. How satisfying to stand in the morning radiance with the words "thank you" singing in our soul.

Creator of the Dawn, fill me at daybreak with gratitude, with a strong sense of your goodness and amazement at the wonder of my life.

PART TWO
THE PRACTICE OF GRATITUDE

I can no other answer make but thanks,
and thanks,
and ever thanks.
        —WILLIAM SHAKESPEARE

16

I thank You God for most this amazing

e. e. cummings

i thank You God for most this amazing
day: for the leaping greenly spirits of trees
and a blue true dream of sky;and for everything
which is natural which is infinite which is yes

(i who have died am alive again today,
and this is the sun's birthday;this is the birth
day of life and of love and wings:and of the gay
great happening illimitably earth)

how should tasting touching hearing seeing
breathing any—lifted from the no
of all nothing—human merely being
doubt unimaginable You?

(now the ears of my ears awake and
now the eyes of my eyes are opened)

Put on the New Self

Colossians 3:1-17

Therefore if you have been raised up with Christ, keep seeking the things above, where Christ is, seated at the right hand of God. Set your mind on the things above, not on the things that are on earth. For you have died and your life is hidden with Christ in God. When Christ, who is our life, is revealed, then you also will be revealed with Him in glory.

Therefore consider the members of your earthly body as dead to immorality, impurity, passion, evil desire, and greed, which amounts to idolatry. For it is because of these things that the wrath of God will come upon the sons of disobedience, and in them you also once walked, when you were living in them. But now you also put them all aside: anger, wrath, malice, slander, and abusive speech from your mouth. Do not lie to one another, since you laid aside the old self with its evil practices, and have put on the new self who is being renewed to a true knowledge according to the image of the One who created him—a renewal in which there is no distinction between Greek and Jew, circumcised and uncircumcised, barbarian, Scythian, slave and freeman, but Christ is all, and in all.

So, as those who have been chosen of God, holy and beloved, put on a heart of compassion, kindness, humility, gentleness and patience; bearing with one another, and forgiving each other, whoever has a complaint against anyone; just as the Lord forgave you, so also should you. Beyond all these things put on love, which is the perfect bond of unity. Let the peace of Christ rule in your hearts, to which indeed you were called in one body; and be thankful. Let the word of Christ richly dwell within you, with all wisdom teaching and admonishing one another with psalms and hymns and spiritual songs, singing with thankfulness in your hearts to God. Whatever you do in word or deed, do all in the name of the Lord Jesus, giving thanks through Him to God the Father.

18

What Does a Grateful Brain Look Like?

Adam Hoffman

"Thank you" doesn't just bring light to people's faces. It also lights up different parts of the brain. Evidence is mounting that gratitude makes a powerful impact on our bodies, including our immune and cardiovascular health. But how does gratitude work in the brain?

A team at the University of Southern California has shed light on the neural nuts and bolts of gratitude in a new study, offering insights into the complexity of this social emotion and how it relates to other cognitive processes.

"There seems to be a thread that runs through subtle acts of gratitude, such as holding a door for someone, all the way up to the big powerful stuff like when someone gives you a kidney," says Glenn Fox, a postdoctoral researcher at USC and lead author of the study. "I designed this experiment to see what aspects of brain function are common to both these small feelings of appreciation and large feelings of gratitude."

In their experiment—which was partially funded by a grant from the Greater Good Science Center's Expanding the Science and Practice of Gratitude project—Fox and his team planned to scan participants' brains while they were feeling grateful to see where gratitude showed up.

But first, they had to induce gratitude. At USC's Shoah Foundation, which houses the world's largest collection of Holocaust testimonies, they pored over hundreds of hours of footage to identify compelling stories of survivors receiving aid from others.

"Many of the survivors talked about receiving life-saving help from other people—from being hidden by strangers during the middle of the Nazi manhunt to being given a new pair of shoes during a wintertime march," says Fox. "And they also talked about less significant gifts, such as bread or a bed at night."

These stories were turned into forty-eight brief vignettes, which the twenty-three experiment participants read while lying in a brain scanner. For example, one said, "A woman at the immigration agency stamps your passport so you can flee to England." For each one, participants were asked to immerse themselves in the context of the Holocaust, imagine how they would feel if they were in the same situation, and then rate how grateful they felt—all while the fMRI machine recorded their brain activity.

The researchers found that grateful brains showed enhanced activity in two primary regions: the anterior cingulate cortex (ACC) and the medial prefrontal cortex (mPFC). These areas have been previously associated with emotional processing, interpersonal bonding and rewarding social interactions, moral judgment, and the ability to understand the mental states of others.

"A lot of people conflate gratitude with the simple emotion of receiving a nice thing. What we found was something a little more interesting," says Fox. "The pattern of [brain] activity we see shows that gratitude is a complex social emotion that is really built around how others seek to benefit us."

In other words, gratitude isn't merely about reward—and doesn't just show up in the brain's reward center. It involves morality, connecting with others, and taking their perspective.

In further studies, Fox hopes to investigate what's going on in the body as gratitude improves our health and well-being.

"It's really great to see all the benefits that gratitude can have, but we are not done yet. We still need to see exactly how it works, when it works, and what are the best ways to bring it out more," he says. "Enhancing our knowledge of gratitude pulls us closer to our own human dignity and what we can do to benefit each other."

19

Dishwashing with Reverence

from *Wind Bell*

This July Brother David was head dishwasher at Tassajara, and before he left he entirely revised the washing ritual and retrained the students. Later, from his home monastery in Western New York, Mount Saviour, he sent the work foreman his suggestions for future dishwashers. They ranged from "a little vinegar in the rinse water makes the glasses sparkle," and "the cats do appreciate the milk left in the glasses from the guest table"; to "We should listen to the sound of the water and the scrubbing, to the various sounds the dishes make when they hit each other. The sounds of our work tell us much about our practice . . . Most people dislike dishwashing. Maybe they can learn to appreciate the touch of the wooden bowls, the pots and mugs and everything they handle, the weight of what we lift up and set down, the various smells and sound. St. Benedict, the Patriarch of Western monks, says that in a monastery every pot and pan should be treated with the same reverence as the sacred vessels on the altar."

20

When Gratitude Becomes a Habit of the Heart

Frank J. Cunningham

I don't know for certain when the ritual started. Very likely in the early winter of 1948 as I was preparing for my First Communion at Midnight Mass that Christmas. It involved a visit to McManus and Riley men's store for my first suit—a white one with short pants.

It was the first of numerous trips to this long-gone business located on the North Side of the first block of State Street in Albany, NY, within sight of the State Capitol building at the top of the hill. "Correct Attire for Gentlemen and Boys" went the store's slogan. It was an era when even a boy needed a proper suit.

So driven by my growth spurts, my mom would steal a Saturday morning from me. Reluctantly I'd ride the bus downtown with her, walk the short distance from the State and Pearl St. stop to the store, and ride the elevator to an upper floor that housed the boys' department. There a familiar gentleman would greet my mom by name and offer his help. On the wall was a rack of boys' suits from small to large and a special section for husky. And a rack of small white suits in an obscure section—McManus and Riley, by virtue of its name, had a brisk business in First Communion suits. Shifting from foot to foot, looking out the windows, and generally wanting to be with my buddies, I'd try on jackets and pants to the soft-spoken cadence of phrases like "will show the dirt," "moderately priced," "good quality," "room to grow" and "alterations included."

Once a suit was agreed on, a tailor would emerge from some mysterious recess in the store, cloth tape-measure draped around his neck, pins in his lapels (yes, he too wore a suit), and a piece of soap with a shaved edge in his hand. I'd stand on a chair and he'd measure and mark the sleeves and pant legs, then waist and crotch. "The suit will be ready for pick-up on Tuesday" he'd say.

By the time I was thirteen years old and had a paper route and a handful of lawn mowing customers, my mom and dad made it clear that purchasing clothes was now my responsibility. So began the savings account and a new strategy for Christmas and birthdays. No more requests for toys. Now I wanted sweaters and shirts as a hedge against having to buy all my clothes. As I got into high school, I began to make the suit purchase by myself. Along with chinos and jeans, ties and shirts, and socks and underwear. Such responsibility may seem harsh these days, but such norms encouraged self-reliance in the neighborhood of my youth.

This was an era when men and women dressed "properly" for nearly all occasions, from baseball games to church. Especially church. My dad was a printer, a tradesman who set type for the local newspapers for fifty-six years, having started his apprenticeship at fourteen. He wore a suit, tie and fedora to church every Sunday. All the dads in the neighborhood did. Ken's dad, a school principal, did. Fran's dad, a postal worker, did. Joe's dad, a banker, did. Ed's dad, a car salesman, did. Little Mike's dad, the synagogue custodian, did. I can't speak with any accuracy about the moms other than that they too "dressed up." You could tell by the hats, the millinery kind. I'd see them all walking to and from St. James on Sunday morning.

I'd also see the dozen or so Jewish men in the neighborhood attired the same way as they walked to evening prayer in the Synagogue at the head of Federal Street, practically in my backyard. Sometimes they would interrupt one of our inventive street ball games and ask one of us to go into the sanctuary to turn on the lights. I'd learn years later that I was a shabbat goy, a gentile asked to do certain tasks that the Torah forbade a pious Jew.

My high school required jackets and ties in all classrooms, a rule we followed with studied indifference. I probably used the same black knit tie for four years. We all left battered sport coats in our lockers till they showed three inches of shirtsleeve and were too tight to button. It was our little rebuke that said "you can insist that we dress as adults, but we'll show you that we're still teenage boys."

I bought my last suit at McManus and Riley when I was eighteen and a senior in high school—a slim cut, three-button roll, dark brown and black, the colors distinguished by a very subtle wale. When I went for a job interview around graduation time, the personal director invited me to sit down with the comment "Nice suit, young man." Important lesson applied.

I got the job but it would last for only the summer,

a brief flirtation with working for several years and delaying my education and saving some money for it. The idea was summarily squashed when my older sister, whom I dearly loved and respected, told me "no way." I was going to college then, no delays. She used a few words for emphasis that I'd never heard her use before. But then she had watched my two older brothers impatiently slip into the Army and Marines, one of them before he finished high school. That decision to go to school shorted me on tuition money, but I was a day-hop student who found work after classes. And I had a nice suit.

In 1959 the jacket and tie was ubiquitous, a near universal dress code, a generations-old expectation. Learning good personal appearance was an important discipline of growing up. My dad taught me how to tie a Windsor knot, how to take care of my shoes, and how to hang my suit properly on a wooden hanger. When my brother Don, twelve years my senior, came back from the Marine Corps in 1953, he showed me how to make a bed tight enough to bounce a quarter off it. More usefully, he taught me to press my pants and shine my shoes. Spit-shine them for that matter. I could see my reflection in the buffed toe-cap. "The Clothes Make the Man," ran one of the popular advertisements of the day. Since we were beginning to discover girls, we felt it probably applied to boys too.

And men could make a respectable living selling clothes. The dad of one of my schoolmates was a familiar face in men's wear at a downtown department store. They did it by building relationships through service and satisfaction. For about a year while in college, I sold men's clothing in the local Montgomery Wards. The full-time salesmen, working on salary and commission, were not to be trifled with. They were adept at picking out the most promising shoppers on the floor—often women shopping for their husbands—and getting to them before we few part-timers had a chance. For them it was a matter of a roof over their heads and food on the table. For us it was just tuition and date money.

It all started to unravel during the 1960's, that beautifully traumatic decade that would quake societal foundations and shake behavioral codes violently. Some were silly and just as well jettisoned. But I wonder about the dress code. Its erosion ultimately led to leisure suits, and how could that have been a good thing?

The changing code was often confusing. In the mid-seventies I interviewed a Manager of the Peninsula Hotel in Hong Kong for a travel piece. At that time High Tea in the Lobby of this elegant hotel called for jacket and tie. But it had become problematic. The hotel gave up on enforcing it when a waiter asked a guest wearing blue jeans and a sport shirt to leave. He was Persian Gulf royalty and not in the least bit happy at being singled out for dismissal.

Like most of my generation I embraced casual wear, even in the workplace and church. As with most changing codes, some folks go to extremes. Although I wear a jacket to church only for weddings, funerals, and maybe Christmas and Easter, I find some churchgoing attire distracting, maybe even lacking reverence and respect. Social norms still make statements about our values.

Are these just easily dismissed musings of an aging man who embraced and/or adapted to his share of changes over the decades? Of course. But it is also an exercise in living out of my memories. It's an exploration of what time has to tell me. Not as navel gazing but as a means of understanding who I am. It's a kind of therapeutic nostalgia, this exploration of the people, events, and customs that shaped us, that helped direct the choices we would make, that helped establish the habits of our hearts.

When I engage in such reflection I often land in a pool of gratitude. For parents with the wisdom to impart self-reliance and respect for things that take hard work to earn; for a sibling with the courage to face down an eighteen-year-old with money in his pocket and the desire to put education on hold; for a brother with the generosity to impart some of the discipline of personal care.

And they are only the hull and keel for this creaking boat. The deck, sails and rigging is a woman who agreed to share her life with me, children who grew up to become good people and loving parents, and a handful of mentors and supporters who saw some promise in me that I hardly saw myself. From them all I learned to chart the course and take the helm.

After all, exploring gratitude becomes a habit of the heart. A habit that fosters the courage to live the last act, the final inning, as completely as possible.

Thank You

*As he entered a village, ten lepers approached him.
Keeping their distance, they called out, saying, "
Jesus, Master, have mercy on us!" When he saw
them, he said to them, "Go and show yourselves
to the priests." And as they went, they were made
clean. Then one of them, when he saw that he
was healed, turned back, praising God with a
loud voice. He prostrated himself at Jesus'feet and
thanked him. And he was a Samaritan. Then Jesus
asked, "Were not ten made clean? But the other
nine, where are they? Was none of them found to
return and give praise to God except this foreigner?"
Then he said to him, "Get up and go on your way;
your faith has made you well."*

—Luke 17:12-19

21

Counting Our Blessings: Why We Say Grace

Anne Lamott

*No matter how you say it, grace can transform
an ordinary meal into a celebration—of family,
love, and gratitude.*

We didn't say grace at our house when I was growing
up because my parents were atheists. I knew even as
a little girl that everyone at every table needed blessing and encouragement, but my family didn't ask
for it. Instead, my parents raised glasses of wine to
the chef: Cheers. Dig in. But I had a terrible secret,
which was that I believed in God, a divine presence
who heard me when I prayed, who stayed close to
me in the dark. So at six years old I began to in-

filtrate religious families like a spy—Mata Hari in plaid sneakers.

One of my best friends was a Catholic girl. Her boisterous family bowed its collective head and said, "Bless us, O Lord, and these thy gifts. . . ." I was so hungry for these words; it was like a cool breeze, a polite thank-you note to God, the silky magnetic energy of gratitude. I still love that line.

I believed that if your family said grace, it meant you were a happy family, all evidence to the contrary. But I saw at certain tables that an improvised grace could cause friction or discomfort. My friend Mark reports that at his big southern childhood Thanksgivings, someone always managed to say something that made poor Granny feel half dead. "It would be along the lines of 'And Lord, we are just glad you have seen fit to keep Mama with us for one more year.' We would all strain to see Granny giving him the fisheye."

I noticed some families shortened the pro forma blessing so they could get right to the meal. If there were more males than females, it was a boy chant, said as one word: "GodisgreatGodisgoodletusthankHimforourfoodAmen." I also noticed that grace usually wasn't said if the kids were eating in front of the TV, as if God refused to listen over the sound of it.

And we've all been held hostage by grace sayers who use the opportunity to work the room, like the Church Lady. But more often, people simply say thank you—we understand how far short we must fall, how selfish we can be, how self-righteous, what brats. And yet God has given us this marvelous meal.

It turns out that my two brothers and I all grew up to be middle-aged believers. I've been a member of the same Presbyterian church for twenty-seven years. My older brother became a born-again Christian— but don't ask him to give the blessing, as it can last forever. I adore him, but your food will grow cold. My younger brother is an unconfirmed but freelance Catholic.

So now someone at our holiday tables always ends up saying grace. I think we're in it for the pause, the quiet thanks for love and for our blessings, before the shoveling begins. For a minute, our stations are tuned to a broader, richer radius. We're acknowledging that this food didn't just magically appear: Someone grew it, ground it, bought it, baked it; wow.

We say thank you for the miracle that we have

stuck together all these years, in spite of it all; that we have each other's backs, and hilarious companionship. We say thank you for the plentiful and outrageous food: Kathy's lox, Robby's *bûche de Noël*. We pray to be mindful of the needs of others. We savor these moments out of time, when we are conscious of love's presence, of Someone's great abiding generosity to our dear and motley family, these holy moments of gratitude. And that is grace.

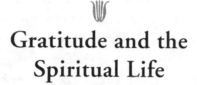

22

Gratitude and the Spiritual Life

James Martin, SJ

The traditional first step of the examen, the end-of-the-day prayer that St. Ignatius Loyola told Jesuits never to omit from their day, is *gratitude*. You recall the good things that happened to you in the past day, and give thanks.

It is an essential step. As David Fleming, SJ, an expert on spirituality, wrote me in a letter, "Ignatius saw the examen as prayer, not just focused on the person, but as directed to God. That's why the examination begins with thanks to God, establishing the focus. It's not simply self-examination or dreamy introspection, it is a way of prayer, a way of being with God."

And Ignatius meant giving thanks for any "benefits," as he said, in the broadest possible sense. Obvious things would include any good news, a tender moment with a spouse, finishing an important project at work. But also less-obvious things: the surprising sight of sunlight on the pavement in the middle of a bleak midwinter's day, the taste of a ham-and-cheese sandwich you had for lunch; satisfaction at the end of a tiring day caring for your children.

For Ignatius many things—no matter how seemingly inconsequential—are occasions for gratitude. You recall them and you "relish" or "savor" them, as Ignatius would say. Savoring is an antidote to our increasingly rushed lives. We live in a busy world, with an emphasis on speed, efficiency and productivity, and we often find ourselves always moving on to the next task at hand. Life becomes an endless series of tasks, and our day becomes a compendium of to-do lists. We become "human doings" instead of "human beings."

Savoring slows us down. In the examen we don't recall an important experience simply to add it to a list of things that we've seen or done; rather, we savor as if we were a wonderful meal. We pause to enjoy what has happened. It's a deepening of our gratitude to God, and reveals the hidden joys of our days. As

Anthony de Mello, SJ, notes, "You sanctify whatever you are grateful for."

The way of Ignatius *celebrates* gratitude. The Spiritual Exercises are crammed with references to expressing gratitude for God's gifts. "I will consider how all good things and gifts descend from above," he writes in the Fourth Week, "from the Supreme and Infinite Power above . . . just as the rays come down from the sun." The examen, as we've mentioned, begins with gratitude. According to John Padberg, SJ, a church historian, for Ignatius the "most execrable and the worst" sin was ingratitude.

Gratitude is an essential element in healthy friendships, too. When I asked my friend Steve, a Jesuit priest in New York, about friendship the first thing he mentioned was the examen. "When I think about friendship, the first thing that comes to mind is finding God in all things," he said. "That surfaces during my examen, when frequently God directs me to things that *God* thinks are important—rather than what I might be focusing on. Often that turns out to be friends and interactions with other Jesuits—in even the simplest of ways: a random comment in a corridor or a homily from another Jesuit. The examen helps me to be more mindful, and more grateful for, my friends."

Paula, a friend who works in campus ministry at a Jesuit school in the Midwest, noted wryly that while everyone will *say* that they are grateful for their friends, the examen makes it easier to focus on that gratitude. "The examen *always* helps in friendships and in family relationships," she said, "because it helps with gratitude." For Sister Maddy, a woman religious who works at a retreat house in Gloucester, Mass., even days when friends aren't as present are occasions for being grateful for them. "Every night during my examen, I remember my gratitude for friends—even if I've not been in contact with them on that particular day. I'm grateful for them wherever they are."

Paul, until recently the rector of a large Jesuit community in Boston, said that gratitude was the most neglected part of friendship. For many years, Paul was in charge of training young Jesuits in Boston and Chicago. He has a lifetime of experience in counseling others in their spiritual lives. "One of the most important parts of friendship is living in gratitude for the gift, and growing into that kind of gratitude," he said.

Paul noted that one common problem in Jesuit friendships stemmed from a lack of gratitude. Without gratitude, you take friendship for granted. "You forget that it takes a little effort. And the small things matter: making time to call, staying in touch. If people can name a friendship, and can appreciate it, they are more inclined to work at it."

True friendships are hard to come by, said Paul, and they take work. And patience. "There are a small number of people who, for whatever reason, easily make and keep friends. But the vast majority of the human race has to ask for friendship, and be patient in waiting for it to come. When we imagine friendships, we tend to imagine things happening instantly. But like anything that's rich and wonderful you grow into it."

But what about those readers for whom talk of friendship reminds them of their loneliness? This discussion may help you find ways to strengthen or deepen your appreciation of relationships with family and friends. But what about the lonely reader? Well, you can enjoy God's friendship in prayer, seeing how God is active in your work, your reading, your hobbies.

Still, what can we say to those who long for a friend?

It would be wrong to downplay the pain of loneliness: I have known many lonely people whose lives are filled with sadness. Perhaps the only thing I could add is to remain open up to the possibility of meeting new friends and not to move to despair, trusting, as much as you can, that God wants you someday to find a friend. The very desire for friendship is an invitation from God to reach out to others. Trust that God desires community for you, though that goal may seem far away.

"For those who wonder why it's not happening faster in their lives," said Paul, "I think that it's more important to love and take the first step. And it also may seem that most people have to spend their lives giving more than receiving," said Paul. "But at the end, even with all the work that is involved, even if you only find one friend in your whole life, it's worth it."

23

I Awaken Before Dawn

Helen Moore

I awaken before dawn, go into the kitchen and
    fix a cup of tea.
I light the candle and sit in its glow on the
    meditation cushion.
Taking my cup in both hands, I lift it to my
    Lord and give thanks.
The feel of the cup against my palms brings the
    potter to mind and I offer a blessing for his
    hands.
I give thanks for the clay, the glaze and the kiln.
I take a sip and follow the warmth into my body.
I offer a blessing for those who brought
    electricity to my home,
who dug the ditches for the lines,
who built my home and put in the wires,

who made my tea kettle and brought me water
    to fill it.
I take a sip and bless the people in India or
    China who grew the tea,
cultivated it, picked and dried the leaves, took it
    to market,
handled it through the many transactions to
    bring it to my home.
I take a sip and bless those people in Florida,
    California or Central America
who grew the tree that blossomed into flowers.
I give thanks for the warmth of the sun and
    the rain which turned the blossoms into
    lemons,
and I bless the hands that picked the fruit,
    sorted it, touched it as it traveled from the
    orchard to my table.
I take another sip and bless the hands of those
    who provided the sugar
which sweetened the tea, harvested the cane,
    processed it, bagged it and sent it on its way
    to me.
I take another sip and lift my cup in gratitude as
    I feel the interconnection of my body now
    with theirs,

my blood now with theirs,
my bones now with theirs,
and my heart fills with love for all of creation.
I give thanks.

24

Unnoticed Prosperity

Joyce Rupp

If you have the ability to read this you are one of the fortunate people on our planet. "Privilege" usually refers to the advantage of easy and ample access to such things as water, food, clothing, shelter, and safety. Instead, I write about something most privileged persons usually do not consider—seven hundred and seventy five million adults on our planet cannot read or write. Of this group, thirty-two million reside in the United States. Countries such as South Sudan have a 73 percent illiteracy rate (www.statisticbrain. com). I discovered this when teaching about "compassion for marginalized persons." As I prepared my notes I became acutely aware of the benefits I received by being able to read what was in front of me. Literacy is such a significant part of my life, yet I had ignored this amazing gift by disregarding what it allowed me to be and to do.

Recently I met with a friend who spoke of being astounded at the amount of get-well cards that "just kept coming" during the months she spent recovering from a serious accident. Then I heard of a married deacon who felt overcome with the love shown him when he looked around at the many who gathered for his ordination. Receiving one get well card or one person coming to a celebration might not catch our attention enough to lead us to overflowing gratitude, but gather together *all* the cards, *all* the people, and something in us finally catches the message of how much there is for which to give thanks.

Just as individual kindness can go unnoticed until a flow of cards arrives, or the support of a community is missed until the crowd gathers for a celebration, the same with literacy. One word, one sentence, one page, might not seem like much, but think of the astounding number of words you've read or written over a lifetime. Imagine just one day when you could not read or write. Consider traveling anywhere without recognizing street signs, unable to comprehend the information on a bank document or a medical notice, incapable of perceiving the message received on a mobile phone, not able to read a Bible verse or a prayer, inept at trying to help with children's homework, bewildered by the food labels in a supermarket and powerless to decipher a recipe.

Do you remember who first helped you to read? Can you recall what it felt like to open a book and actually pronounce and understand the words on the page? Perhaps reading did not come easily for you or you had difficulty due to poor eyesight. Or you may be someone who read at an early age and has never stopped relishing the gift. Each of us has our own story of becoming literate. It's a story that helped shape us into the person we are today. What would life have been like for you if you had never been able to read?

Take a moment to look closely at the individual pieces of your life and recognize the abundance. Literacy is one of the valued possessions that contributes to that prosperity. What small things might you have overlooked? What individual gifts can you gather as a whole and see with new eyes? What awesome privileges and opportunities do you take for granted?

25

A Discipline

Henri Nouwen

In the past I always thought of gratitude as a spontaneous response to the awareness of gifts received, but now I realize that gratitude can also be lived as a discipline. The discipline of gratitude is the explicit effort to acknowledge that all I am and have is given to me as a gift of love, a gift to be celebrated with joy.

Gratitude as a discipline involves a conscious choice. I can choose to be grateful even when my emotions and feelings are still steeped in hurt and resentment. It is amazing how many occasions present themselves in which I can choose gratitude instead of a complaint. I can choose to be grateful when I am criticized, even when my heart still responds in bitterness. I can choose to speak about goodness and beauty, even when my inner eye still looks for someone to accuse or something to call ugly. I can choose to listen to the voices that forgive and to look at the faces that smile, even while I still hear words of revenge and see grimaces of hatred.

There is always the choice between resentment and gratitude because God has appeared in my darkness, urged me to come home, and declared in a voice filled with affection: "You are with me always, and all I have is yours." Indeed, I can choose to dwell in the darkness in which I stand, point to those who are seemingly better off than I, lament about the many misfortunes that have plagued me in the past, and thereby wrap myself up in my resentment. But I don't have to do this. There is the option to look into the eyes of the one who came out to search for me and see therein that all I am and all I have is pure gift calling for gratitude.

The choice for gratitude rarely comes without some real effort. But each time I make it, the next choice is a little easier, a little freer, a little less self-conscious. Because every gift I acknowledge reveals another and another until finally, even the most normal, obvious, and seemingly mundane event or encounter proves to be filled with grace. There is an Estonian proverb that says: "Who does not thank for little will not thank for much." Acts of gratitude make one grateful because, step by step, they reveal that all is grace.

Thank Yous

Got no check books, got no banks.
Still I'd like to express my thanks—
I got the sun in the mornin' and the moon at night.
—IRVING BERLIN

Let us be grateful to people who make us happy;
they are the charming gardeners who make our
souls blossom.
—MARCEL PROUST

26

"They Had Caught a Great Number of Fish and Their Nets Were Tearing"

Carol Howard Merritt

I leaned my head against the metal window of the bus. The soggy rice fields passed before the glass, and I wondered how the men, women, and children could work while keeping their hats balanced on their heads. Their strong backs bestowed them with exceptional grace. I imagined that it would be a good day of work, with the beauty of the hills surrounding them.

Then, as if traveling through time, bicycles filled the street and fields turned into grey concrete and metal factories. The workers changed jobs as we moved from rural to urban landscapes, from agricultural farmers to industrial workers.

I was fifteen, on a mission trip. There are a lot of questions these days about the nature of these trips. Too often, American teenagers think that they are somehow saving people in other cultures, while people from other countries are just putting up with the oddities of our privilege.

I see the concerns, but I'm thankful that I had a chance to go overseas. My parents would have never allowed me to venture out of the country for a vacation or an educational trip, but for a mission trip they would. And so I slept in tents in a field in Switzerland, on pews in a houseboat in Hong Kong, and in clay huts in Africa. I traveled the world, under the guise of saving people.

Of course, as those things went, they were saving me. Each country gave me a different sense of proportion. It is one thing to sit in your cushy living room and see the images of little children with swarming flies and bloated bellies looking at you with big glassy eyes. You can turn the television off and walk away. You can allow the image to quickly fade. But it's an entirely different thing to be a college student, playing soccer with kids on a Tuesday afternoon. They show up without any shoes and you know that they have not eaten anything all day. Those friendly eyes keep their gaze as the inequities in our globe become quite clear.

The mission trips gave me the gift of proportion, even though I felt like my culture shock came with covetous whiplash-moving from want to revulsion. I had to fight becoming a complete social misfit. I sat with my friends as we compared the label of our designer jeans, scanned the pages of *Elle*, and assessed where we were on the fashion totem pole. I wanted the shiny products as much as my friends, even though I couldn't shake the memory of the family living on rice that they harvested from their small field.

Of course, it's easy to look back at my life as an American teen and point at my shallowness. Teenagers are particularly susceptible to marketing manipulation, and we allow corporations to relentlessly communicate to our adolescents how inept they are because of their lack of material goods. I was no exception.

But it didn't stop there. As we grew older, it wasn't only about the labels on our clothes, but about the car. Then it became about the position we held or the amount of power we could wield. It became about how well we married and what sort of real estate we acquired. We were still playing the same game, just with different prizes.

No walk of life seems to be immune to the comparisons. I once heard a colleague comment with great pretention about the company another pastor used to take his portrait photo. Ministers compare how big our steeples are, usually by assessing the size of our congregations, the value of the buildings, or the location of the church. When we meet each other, we ask benign questions as we assess our abundance compared to the next person.

In all of it, we become so sensitive to the manufactured needs that surround us until we are unable to grasp what we have. Even in our churches, we've lost our sense of abundance. We look at the budgets of past decades and see decline. We might even have an endowment, but all we can focus on is how much we lost. We look at our buildings, focus on the cracks, and dream about the next construction project. We become numb to the soaring artistry or acres of land. We simply echo that we do not have enough until our myths of scarcity become excuses for not feeding the hungry, sheltering the homeless, and working for the reign of God.

In each phase, in each walk of life, we become

consumed by what we do not have and we lose the amazement of what God has given to us.

Yet, we can learn it again from the disciples who pulled up their nets and saw them bursting with shimmering, restless fish. They were amazed by what God had given them. When we pull up our nets, do we only see what we do not have? We've lost our astonishment, because we can only think, "We had more fish before the recession. Remember when the greatest generation filled our pews with entire families? We had so many more fish back then. Those were the days!"

The disciples remind us to live lives of astonished gratitude for all God has given to us. In the years to come, may we set aside our careful attention to our losses, and may we learn to be amazed with all that God has given to us.

To the glory of God our Creator, God our Liberator, and God our Sustainer. Amen.

Glenn, the Mayor of Woodhaven, On the Importance of Gratitude in Life

Terrance W. Klein

Years ago, after my father had lost the grocery store and had gone to work as a custodian at the parish, he would discuss his day at the dinner table. People used to do that. I should have paid more attention because he was usually talking about something that had broken down, something I've now inherited.

Remember how, sometimes, things could get so bad that Batman had to call upon Superman, or vice-a-versa? The hero of my father's story was always Glenn Breford, a local heating and air conditioning man. Dad quoted Glenn like folks quote Genesis: Glenn says those filters need to be changed every autumn; Glenn said you can't run compressors at that level for that long. Glenn may not have been a superhero, but he was definitely the one to call when something went wrong in our little Gotham.

Let's move forward, about thirty years. Dad has been gone for seventeen years, and Glenn is now the Mayor of Woodhaven, the local nursing home. It's not an elected position. It's a title I've given him.

Visiting residents of a nursing home, as a group, before and after Mass, is a lot like visiting the second grade. You're never sure who is going to speak, and you're rather certain that each will begin talking before the first person finished. Another similarity, you're not always sure what you've just heard, but it's heartfelt.

Glenn carries an oxygen tank with him now. I asked him about it. "Some doctor in league with oxygen tank salesmen. I don't need it." Every week, either before Mass, or after Mass, Glenn rises from his chair, tank in tow, and comes up to me at the altar and to say, rather solemnly, "Father, we want to thank you for coming to say Mass for us."

"You're welcome, Glenn." That's either not the right response or it's insufficient, because Glenn typically repeats the expression of gratitude, as though he wanted the local press to hear and to record it. "No, we are very grateful." Clearly, it matters a great deal to Glenn that I know this. Learn to watch for gratitude, in yourself and others.

"Hear this, you who trample upon the needy and destroy the poor of the land!" says the Lord through the Prophet Amos, "The Lord has sworn by the pride of Jacob: Never will I forget a thing they have done!" (8: 4, 7).

Some say that talk of money doesn't belong in the pulpit. Some have a long list of what doesn't belong in the pulpit, and not without some point, I might add. But it's hard to say that our relationship with money has nothing to do with our relationship to God, not when Jesus warns us that:

> No servant can serve two masters.
> He will either hate one and love the other,
> or be devoted to one and despise the other.
> You cannot serve both God and mammon
>
> (Lk 16: 13)

Sometimes preachers need to ask for money, and they shouldn't be ashamed to do so. Money makes the world go round, as they say. It pays for heating and air conditioning.

Yet there's a lesson deeper than stewardship here. Ideally, we ought to reverence God and owe money to no one. But many of us reverence money, and we owe it to just about everybody, especially credit card companies. Leave the words of Amos to deal with the credit card companies. What about us?

Why do so many of us Americans spend beyond our means? Why do we indebt ourselves and then try, as much as possible, to ignore those who are genuinely in need: the poor ones of the nation who don't choose, or create, their lot? Many, too poor to have a credit card.

Remember Glenn, the Mayor of Woodhaven? A little excessive in his thanks? Earlier this week, I stood for several minutes and watched a nearly full moon pass in and out of dark clouds. How beautiful! How much would people pay to see such a sight, if heaven charged for its blessings? What if cats charged us to be petted, or dogs wanted a dollar for each lick they gave?

The best things in life really are free. Take a walk through nature. Watch leaves turn color and fall. Look up at the moon or the sun. What would people pay to see a rainbow, if it came with a price tag? Watch a child open a present. Watch a nursing home resident receive Holy Communion. Then, consider the list of things you've bought on credit with your cards.

How does it happen that the best in life is free and that we take it for granted? Why do we spend money, which we don't have, on things, which we don't need, when so many around the world, and in our neighborhoods, go hungry? For them, the best things in life—housing, health care and food—aren't free. They're denied. What does it mean to tell a child without fresh water to enjoy the sun?

St. John of the Cross suggested that the first movement of an authentic spiritual life wasn't an acknowledgment of sin. That's probably second. The first movement of the spiritual life is gratitude: an awareness that all of nature, all the world, all of life comes to us as gift. It need not be. We need not be.

People like Glenn, the Mayor of Woodhaven, have a lot to teach us. There are two ways to look at the world: seeing what you can get out of it or to recognizing what you've been given in it.

A Golden Cloud
Helen Phillips, MM

Walking alone in the cool autumn air, I was struck by the kaleidoscope of color all around me!—reds, oranges, yellows, browns—so many varieties, shades, hues! It was absolutely breathtaking! Where to look? How to absorb all this?

Walking further along the path I entered deeper into the woods. Here I was surrounded by trees on all sides. There was a deep silence. Nothing stirred. The trees were covered almost without exception with bright lemon-colored leaves. I stood stock still in the midst of this overwhelming beauty, this painted air! I raised my mind and heart *and my head* to God. As I looked directly above me I felt absorbed into a golden cloud glistening in the rays of sunlight sprinkled among the leaves. Speechless was I!

God was present in His creation, and He was sharing this with me! This was His gift to me!

Praise God for His wonderful majesty, Alleluia!

Thanksgiving for the Lord's Saving Goodness

Psalm 118

Give thanks to the LORD, for He is good;
　　For His lovingkindness is everlasting.
Oh let Israel say,
　　"His lovingkindness is everlasting."
Oh let the house of Aaron say,
　　"His lovingkindness is everlasting."
Oh let those who fear the LORD say,
　　"His lovingkindness is everlasting."
From my distress I called upon the LORD;
　　The LORD answered me and set me in a
　　large place.
The LORD is for me; I will not fear;
　　What can man do to me?
The LORD is for me among those who help me;
　　Therefore I will look with satisfaction on

those who hate me.
It is better to take refuge in the Lord
>Than to trust in man.
It is better to take refuge in the Lord
>Than to trust in princes.
All nations surrounded me;
>In the name of the Lord I will surely cut
>them off.
They surrounded me, yes, they surrounded me;
>In the name of the Lord I will surely cut
>them off.
They surrounded me like bees;
>They were extinguished as a fire of thorns;
>In the name of the Lord I will surely cut
>them off.
You pushed me violently so that I was falling,
>But the Lord helped me.
The Lord is my strength and song,
>And He has become my salvation.
The sound of joyful shouting and salvation is in
>the tents of the righteous;
>The right hand of the Lord does valiantly.
The right hand of the Lord is exalted;
>The right hand of the Lord does valiantly.
I will not die, but live,

And tell of the works of the LORD.
The LORD has disciplined me severely,
>   But He has not given me over to death.
Open to me the gates of righteousness;
>   I shall enter through them, I shall give
>   thanks to the LORD.
This is the gate of the LORD;
>   The righteous will enter through it.
I shall give thanks to You, for You have answered
me,
>   And You have become my salvation.
The stone which the builders rejected
>   Has become the chief corner stone.
This is the LORD's doing;
>   It is marvelous in our eyes.
This is the day which the LORD has made;
>   Let us rejoice and be glad in it.
O LORD, do save, we beseech You;
>   O LORD, we beseech You, do send
>   prosperity!
Blessed is the one who comes in the name of the
LORD;
>   We have blessed you from the house of the
>   LORD.
The LORD is God, and He has given us light;

Bind the festival sacrifice with cords to the
horns of the altar.
You are my God, and I give thanks to You;
You are my God, I extol You.
Give thanks to the LORD, for He is good;
For His lovingkindness is everlasting.

Five Inspirational Ways to Gain Greater Gratitude

Kelli Wheeler

It's just a fact of life: sometimes, for whatever reason, it's hard to be grateful for what we have. And just because it's November, a month marked by a national holiday devoted to giving thanks, doesn't mean we will all of a sudden have the capacity to be grateful—especially if life is currently taking great pleasure in putting challenges in your path.

When I find myself in a dark place, my motivation and appreciation snuffed out, a good inspirational quote is a flint that sparks a tinder of hope in me—reigniting my fire to be a positive force in this world.

In my opinion, there is no better caster of flints than Mother Teresa. Nearly two decades after her death her enlightenment and wisdom still resonates in our tumultuous world. So if you're feeling less than grateful this Thanksgiving, try the five ideas below, illustrated with inspirational quotes from Mother Teresa, to kick-start your gratitude and positive attitude.

1. *Change your perspective.*
   "Yesterday is gone. Tomorrow has not yet come. We have only today. Let us begin."
   —*Mother Teresa*

The easiest thing to change about yourself is your perspective. With daily stresses and normal frustrations it's easy to fall into a rut of thinking negatively. My husband once stopped me mid-rant asking, "Do you ever have anything positive to say?" Only then did I hear myself. I was horrified. When had I turned into such a negative person? From then on I made a point to lead with the positive and shelve the negative. Helping to cement the habit I imagined waking up each morning without anything I didn't thank God for the night before. Illuminating your life with that perspective, it becomes easy to see and be grateful for the gifts in this life.

Each sunrise is the promise of rewriting your story. Why not make it a positive one?

2. *Interact with people.*

> "Let no one ever come to you without leaving
> better and happier. Be the living expression of
> God's kindness: kindness in your face, kind-
> ness in your eyes, kindness in your smile."
>
> —*Mother Teresa*

Have you ever complimented a stranger out of the blue? It's great! You almost always get a surprised, delighted smile and a "Thank you." Such simple kindness spreads reciprocal joy and gratitude—it feels good for both of you. I try to give a stranger a compliment at least once a day.

I'll tell the woman in front of me in the grocery line that I like her shoes. Or I'll tell a frazzled mother how well-mannered her child is. I'll tell a checker at Target that I think he's doing a great job moving the line along. If you have the opportunity to put a smile on someone's face, why be stingy with it?

Even a smile is a simple way to make kindness contagious. Easy to give; easy to receive. No strings attached to have a human connection that fosters gratitude.

3. *Do good works.*

> "God doesn't require us to succeed, he only
> requires that you try."
>
> —*Mother Teresa*

Like giving a smile, giving a helping hand does wonders for the soul. I once was going about my normal routine with my dreaded stop at the gym—the necessity becoming a drudgery. I was hustling to leave the locker room when I noticed an elderly woman having great trouble with the normally simple act of putting on a sock and shoe. I stopped to help her. Her profuse gratitude over something that struck me as common courtesy made me feel like a superhero. It made me want to do more good works—realizing how a simple gesture to one person could be something profound to another.

I left the gym feeling good not because I forced myself to work out, but because I took the time to look beyond myself to see and help others in need. And a binary effect? Helping someone physically challenged made me grateful for my own good health and that I shouldn't take my ability to work out for granted!

4. *Focus on family and friends.*

"What can you do to promote world peace?
Go home and love your family."
—*Mother Teresa*
I may not be able to personally get the kidnapped

schoolgirls back from Nigeria, but I can create a loving and supporting environment for my daughter. The person I voted for may not have won office, but I can tell my son after a rough game that I love watching him play sports no matter who wins. I can't stop religious persecution in the Middle East, but I can bring my friend a hot meal for her family while her son's in the hospital.

Sometimes making a difference in the world just means making a difference in someone's life. A high tide raises all boats, so why not make it a tidal wave of love and support that surges from our own shores?

5. *Love yourself.*

> "Be faithful in small things because it is in them that your strength lies."
>
> —*Mother Teresa*

As a busy mother of two teenagers trying to keep our lives, a career, and our home afloat, sometimes I feel like I have given so much for others that I have nothing left of myself. It is in those times, when I feel like I'm running on fumes, that I fill up my tank.

I take myself to the movies. I get a big buttery bag of popcorn. I get a giant cup of root beer. And I open a jumbo box of Junior Mints. I don't need to jet off to the Bahamas (as if I could). I don't need someone to tell me how wonderful I am (though that's always nice). I don't need a grand gesture to make me feel appreciated (but feel free to try). I just remember that while I'm busy giving out love, support and happiness . . . I have to save a little for myself too.

There is no better way to get in touch with your gratitude than to be thankful for you.

Thank Yous

Saying thank you is more than good manners. It is good spirituality. —ALFRED PAINTER

We learned about gratitude and humility—that so many people had a hand in our success, from the teachers who inspired us to the janitors who kept our school clean . . . and we were taught to value everyone's contribution with respect.
—MICHELLE OBAMA

I thank Thee first because I was never robbed before; second, because although they took my purse they did not take my life; third, although they took my all, it was not much; and fourth, because it was I who was robbed and not I who robbed.
—MATTHEW HENRY

31

Messenger

Mary Oliver

My work is loving the world.
Here the sunflowers, there the hummingbird—
    equal seekers of sweetness.
Here the quickening yeast; there the blue plums.
Here the clam deep in the speckled sand.

Are my boots old? Is my coat torn?
Am I no longer young, and still not half-perfect? Let me
    keep my mind on what matters,
which is my work,

which is mostly standing still and learning to be
    astonished.
The phoebe, the delphinium.

The sheep in the pasture, and the pasture.
Which is mostly rejoicing, since all the ingredients are here,

which is gratitude, to be given a mind and a heart
        and these body-clothes,
a mouth with which to give shouts of joy
        to the moth and the wren, to the sleepy dug-up clam,
telling them all, over and over, how it is
        that we live forever.

32

Gratefulness: A Source of Strength

Dietrich Bonhoeffer

First:

Nothing can console us when we lose a beloved person and no one should try. We have to simply bear and survive it. That sounds hard but is in fact a great consolation: When the hole remains unfilled, we remain connected through it. It is wrong to say that God fills the gap, because he keeps it empty and so helps us to sustain our old communion, even through pain.

Then:

The more beautiful and fulfilling our memories, the harder the separation. But gratefulness transforms the agony of memory into a quiet joy. We should avoid burrowing in our memories, just as we do not look at a precious gift continuously. Rather, we should save them for special hours, like a hidden treasure of which we are certain. Then a pervading joy and strength will flow from the past.

33

Attitude of Gratitude

Harijot Singh Khalsa

Once there were two students. One day they were both told that they had received the great honor of seeing the Grandmaster. They were both very excited and humbled by this honor. The two students hiked to a remote mountain top to a very beautiful temple there. Both students were excited to see the Grandmaster.

The junior student volunteered himself to go first, and he entered in to the master's chamber. The Grandmaster looked very calm . . . and silent . . . . His eyes showed kindness. The Grandmaster said, "Look in the Mystical Window and see the Truth." The junior student looked, and after a while he had a vision. He saw himself holding The Sacred Sword and also holding The Sacred Book. He told the master, "I looked just like the paintings of the saints of old! It was amazing!"

The Grandmaster said, "Yes indeed." Then the student said, "If I am like the saints of old . . . then I must be a very great person!" The Grandmaster assured him, "Indeed, you are very special to God." The student decided that because he was so special, that he must go and teach others. The junior student left the chamber very excited, saying, "I knew it! I was always treated like a junior student, as if I don't know anything, but I AM A GREAT MAN! Everyone should listen to everything I say. I WILL GO AND TEACH THESE PEOPLE!!!" After he left to teach, the Grandmaster sighed to himself and said, "Indeed you shall."

The senior student was now called to see the master and told to look in to the Mystical Window to see the truth. Calmly, she looked in the window. After a while she shared her vision, "Master, I saw myself holding The Sacred Sword in one hand and The Sacred Book in another hand." She explained how in the vision she looked like the saints of old. The Grandmaster said, "Indeed." "Master, if the truth is that I am like the saints of old, then does that mean I am a great woman?" The Grandmaster assured her just as he had the junior student, "Indeed you are, you are very special to God." Then the student asked, "If I am a great woman, if I am special to God, if I am like the saints of old . . . doesn't that mean it is my task to spread the truth?" The Grandmaster said, "Yes indeed it does."

Then the senior student did something the junior student didn't do . . . the senior student thought for a moment . . . and asked, "Master, may I ask, I've always seen the saints holding the Sacred Book and Sword . . . what do these things really mean?" The Grandmaster was very pleased, "Ah! It means God has given us all very many gifts but it takes a lot of focus to constantly remember what has been given to us. It takes focus . . . as sharp as a SWORD!" The student was amazed to hear the meaning of the Sword, "So it means we have to focus at each moment to remember all the gifts God has given us!!" The Grandmaster continued to teach her, "Indeed! And once you focus and remember the gifts . . . it takes the heart of a poet to fully appreciate them. The Sacred Book is like flowing poetry."

The senior student again did something the junior student didn't do. She started breathing deeply. She began to meditate . . . "I am using my sword-like focus to remember every blessing the universe has given me. . . . My heart is melting and I wish to sing the praises of the Infinite forever, and then sing them even more!" As she was meditating she realized she was using The Sacred Book AND Sword, "Right now, I am using sword-focus and my heart is flowing like poetry on the pages of a book!" The Grandmaster was extremely pleased. Bursting with love for his student, he said, "Indeed you ARE!"

Later both the students came down the mountain.

In town, the people really wanted to know if the Grandmaster had revealed the truth of the whole universe to them. The junior student came jogging down the mountain, very excited. With his eyes wide he yelled, "LISTEN TO ME, LISTEN TO ME!" The people asked, "Oh my goodness! Did the Grandmaster bless you?" "Did you look in the Mystical Window? What did you see?" The junior student shouted, "THE GRANDMASTER PRAISED ME AS A GREAT MAN!" The people were astonished. The junior student continued, "The Mystical Window revealed that I AM THE GREAT SAINT OF THIS AGE! It is I who has The Sacred Sword and I who has The Sacred Word." He continued telling them his ideas. What he said sounded very much like the truth, and many people who heard him believed everything he said.

Soon he became very famous and he had many followers.

The senior student came down the mountain smiling and humming happily to herself, "Hmmmmmh-hhhmmmmhhmmm . . ." The few people who didn't follow the first student noticed something. The senior student seemed very peaceful . . . very content. They asked, "Well, what did you see?" The senior student said, "I saw that God has given all of us many gifts." She smiled with kindness. People wanted to hear more, so she taught them, "There are two things. One is the challenge of remembering our gifts. As the other is the heart to never forget them." Those who heard this felt calm and bright, and they smiled. The senior student continued on her way, the people still wanted to hear more from her, "Where are you going? What will you do?" She smiled with kindness, "Oh, I'll go somewhere and do something, that's not what matters. The real challenge is to remember God's blessings and then to never forget." The people smiled again.

Those who followed the junior student started their own religion. They worshipped the junior student as a prophet and a saint. Those who followed the senior student just fell in love with life. They were full of gratitude and spent their lives happily serving everyone they met.

A constant attitude of gratitude brings every blessing in life.

Steps of Gratitude

Jim Wallis

I didn't know much about sepsis until it hit me out of the blue the Friday before Thanksgiving. After working late Thursday night, I woke up the next morning shivering and shaking, with my teeth rattling and full of pain; my left leg was swollen and fire-engine red.

I was immediately sent to the hospital and told frightening things about how dangerous a septic cellulitis infection can be. The ailment is random and can strike people of all ages; bacteria gets under the skin and spreads, and if it goes into the blood stream, things can get dangerous indeed.

I am certainly not used to lying in a hospital with intravenous antibiotics being pumped into me day and night. Fortunately, thanks to my overall good health, I responded quickly to the antibiotics, resulting in a full recovery. I've often visited others in hospitals and been an advocate for patients in bureaucratic health-care systems, and this unexpected visit reminded me why that is so important. It is easy to feel alone in those systems and to lose your voice. I have always been impressed by nurses, who so often bring life, laughter, and even love to health systems that so easily block out such things, and some of my nurses were the delight of my lockdown hospital time.

I grew close to my roommate in the hospital, a man who, like me, is married to an English woman, and who was clearly suffering from cardiac issues. The lack of privacy through flimsy curtains forced me to overhear a doctor telling him that he had two choices: a heart surgery that the doctor thought the man wouldn't survive, or hospice care with only six months or less to live.

Decisions about life and death often suddenly fill these hospital rooms. My leg infection quickly shrank in comparison, and being present to my roommate and his wife became very important. Friends coming by to talk to my roommate brought tears, stories, smiles, and fears.

Two weeks before entering the hospital, I had gone on a much needed personal retreat—not to lead but just to listen, learn, and be quiet. The topics of the seminar were "character" and "gratitude." The former was intriguing, as the subject of character always is to me. But I found the latter theme, gratitude, to be profoundly challenging—and restful at the same time. Gratitude is hard. It is especially hard for those of us who see their vocation as changing the world—seeing what is wrong and trying to make it right. We see the unjust things and want to make them just, the broken things and want to help heal them; we see the bad and want the good. It can be exhausting.

Our retreat leader talked about the Vietnamese Buddhist monk Thich Nhat Hanh, a well-known poet and peace activist now living in France, who travels internationally and teaches meditation. We were taught his meditation of walking with steps of gratitude—each time one's feet touch the earth, the step is accompanied by a prayer of gratitude.

Then we were sent out to walk, to feel our feet touching the ground and to remember things we were grateful for. The first things were easy for me—my boys, Luke and Jack, my wife, Joy. My mom and dad and the rest of my family. Longtime friends and companions on this journey. The community at Sojourners that carries out our mission and the extended community around the country and the world that supports us and works with us in so many ways.

Then it began to grow. Instead of thinking of the many things wrong with the world, the things I want to change, I kept putting my mind and heart on the people and things for which I am grateful. It started to relax, settle, and focus me, as our retreat director said it would.

Then I got sepsis a couple weeks later. In the midst of the pain, weakness, and fear, I remembered the things for which I am most grateful. I came home from the hospital two days before Thanksgiving feeling deep appreciation for all the blessings in my life.

More and more, I am coming to see how a regular meditation of gratitude for this world and for the people in it may well be the best way of preparing and sustaining me every day to work to change the things that still must be changed. It made me realize once again how grateful I am to all the people who keep our mission at Sojourners going each and every day.

We have much further to go, but I am so thankful that we're on this journey together.

35

Shine On, Farmer Boy

Bishop James E. Walsh, MM
For the People of China

Shine on, farmer boy, symbol to me of the thousand million like you who drew the Son of God from heaven to smooth and bless your weary anxieties and your puzzled brows. Come to me often in your barefoot squalor and look at me from out of those hopeless and bewildered eyes. Do not let me forget that vision, but stay by me and preside over my dreams. Teach me that souls are people. And remind me everlastingly that they are magnificent people like you.

Thank Yous

Gratitude is the memory of the heart.
— Jean Baptiste Massieu

Thanks for the memory.

— Bob Hope

36

I Will Treasure Your Letter

J. K. Rowling

In September of 2006, following a desperately sad child-hood that saw both drug-addicted parents murdered and the care of her younger siblings left in her hands, sixteen-year-old Sacia Flowers decided to write to J. K. Rowling and thank her for creating Harry Potter, her "best friend" during the most difficult of times. Her letter can be read below, followed by Rowling's lovely, encouraging response.

Sept. 2, 2006
Dear Mrs. Rowling,

I have so much I'd like to say, but I know you are a very busy woman so I'll try to keep it short and not take up too much of your time. Primarily, I would like to say

I absolutely LOVE your books and have at least one copy of each on my book shelf, in addition to Harry's school books for Comic Relief and several analytical and biographical ones related to Harry and you. With that, I'll just go right into it. I first heard of the Harry Potter series when I was in fourth grade, but at the time I was not much of a reader. In the beginning of my fifth grade year, I went out on a whim and began Sorcerer's Stone; I was hooked by page three and have not been seen without a book on hand since.

I have never enjoyed a series as much as I have every one of your Harry books. I noticed, as I read each of the six books the first time through, I was the same age as Harry, which was quite coincidental. I have cried at least once reading every one of the six so far (several times during a few) and out right bawled at the end of Half-Blood Prince. Losing Dumbledore, empathizing with Harry and his friends, seeing their heartache, and feeling as though I had lost a grandpa myself was utterly overwhelming. The relationship that evolved and grew between Harry and Dumbledore from the end of book five and throughout book six increased the intensity of this for me.

This emotional reaction, I speculate, may perhaps be a result of the strong connection I feel with Harry.

Not only do I wear glasses and have green eyes, thus sharing a bit of his physical appearance (I realize I speak of Harry as if he is a real person, but to me he is very real indeed, as I'm sure he is to you), but I'm also an orphan, both parents having been murdered when I was younger. In addition, I was always picked on before I went to my new school, as Harry was by Dudley and his cronies before he went to Hogwarts. So, I also have a strong emotional understanding with Harry and feel the severity of Harry's loss of Sirius (I bawled here as well); for these reasons Harry holds a special place in my heart and he always will.

Being picked on most of my life, I never had many friends due to my own insecurities and fear of loss, but through the most difficult times in my life, Harry was my best friend when I needed him most and he lent me his world in which to escape my own grief and hurt, and for this I thank you from the deepest part of my heart. To me, it's like Harry and I grew up together. I have grown a lot emotionally over the years and am now sixteen (as is Harry). Thank you so very much for lending me your hero and his world. He is my hero, and you are my heroine.

I do not expect a reply, as I know you are a very busy woman, mother, and wife, but I do hope you have a chance to read this letter (I understand you have a plethora of fan mail and there's only so many hours in the day). I do not wish for you to read this or reply so I can brag about making contact with a celebrity or something ridiculous of that nature; in fact, my family will probably not even know that I wrote to you. Mostly I just really wanted to express my deepest gratitude and appreciation to you and Harry. I needed for you to know how important he has been to me.

Thank you, for everything.

Most Sincerely,

Sacia (Say-sha) Flowers

JK Rowling

19th September 2006

Dear Sacia (beautiful name, I've never heard it before),

Thank you for your incredible letter; incredible, because you do indeed sound phenomenally like Harry Potter, in your physical resemblance and in your life experience. I cannot tell you how moved I was by what you wrote, nor how sorry I am to hear about your parents. What a terrible loss.

I know what it is like to be picked on, as it happened to me, too, throughout my adolescence. I can only wish that you have the same experience that I did, and become happier and more secure the older you get. Being a teenager can be completely horrible, and many of the most successful people I know felt the same way. I think the problem is that adolescence, though often misrepresented as a time of rebellion and unconventionality, actually requires everybody to conform if they aspire to popularity—or at least to "rebel" while wearing the "right" clothes! You're now standing on the threshold of a very different phase in your life, one where you are much more likely to find kindred spirits, and much less likely to be subject to the pressures of your teenage years.

It is an honor to me to know that somebody like you loves Harry as much as you do. Thank you very much for writing to me, I will treasure your letter (which entitles you to boast about this response as much as you like!)

With lots of love,

JK Rowling

(Jo to you!)

x

37

An Alleluia Heart

Joan Chittister

Gratitude is not only the posture of praise but it is also the basic element of real belief in God.

When we bow our heads in gratitude, we acknowledge that the works of God are good. We recognize that we cannot, of ourselves, save ourselves. We proclaim that our existence and all its goods come not from our own devices but are part of the works of God. Gratitude is the alleluia to existence, the praise that thunders through the universe as tribute to the ongoing presence of God with us even now.

Thank you for the new day.

Thank you for this work.

Thank you for this family.

Thank you for our daily bread.

Thank you for this storm and the moisture it brings to a parched earth.

Thank you for the corrections that bring me to growth.

Thank you for the bank of crown vetch that brings color to the hillside.

Thank you for the pets that bind us to nature.

Thank you for the necessities that keep me aware of your bounty in my life.

Without doubt, unstinting gratitude saves us from the sense of self-sufficiency that leads to forgetfulness of God.

Praise is not an idle virtue in life. It says to us, "Remember to whom you are indebted. If you never know need, you will come to know neither who God is nor who you yourself are."

Need is what tests our trust. It gives us the opportunity to allow others to hold us up in our weakness, to realize that only God in the end is the measure of our fullness.

Once we know need, we are better human beings. For the first time we know solidarity with the poorest of the poor. We become owners of the pain of the world and devote ourselves to working on behalf of those who suffer.

Finally, it is need that shows us how little it takes to be happy.

Once we know all of those things, we have come face-to-face with both creation and the Creator. It is the alleluia moment that discovers both God and goodness for us.

Let us learn to come to prayer with an alleluia heart so that our prayer can be sincere.

38

Six Inches Off the Ground

William J. O'Malley, SJ

Good times and bum times, I've seen 'em all
And, my dear, I'm still here.
—STEPHEN SONDHEIM

Gratitude's one of the most difficult virtues. Generosity's actually easier. So are patience, fortitude, even chastity. When we have a firm grip on those virtues, there's a kind of righteous kickback; it says, "See? I'm not such a bad sort after all." But gratitude's, well, a debt, imposed by a kindness emanating from outside ourselves: someone pitching in with the dishes when we're all alone at the sink, someone showing up at the hospital bedside when we really thought suffering alone was more noble, someone bestowing existence on us when we didn't exist and could do nothing to have deserved such an invitation.

When we've been graced, it behooves us to be grace full. Grateful.

But for many people, especially those of us who've been around awhile, gratitude's not an opportunity to rejoice and be more generous, just another word for "indebtedness," and nobody likes bills. Bills have been our stories' antagonists since before we left school. We don't socialize with pawnbrokers and bookies. Debt's a condition we'd just as soon not be reminded of. It makes us feel almost . . . guilty. Best thing to do is just stow that sense of indebtedness in some attic in our minds, and maybe it can become less bothersome. We admit it's real but . . . out of the way.

And yet it's a fact that won't go away. We're all indebted—to our mothers for carrying us around nine months and risking death so we could live, to our fathers for being flinty places against which to hone our adulthood. Who was the teacher who taught us to read, who refused to accept swamp-gas essays? Who reached out to us in our anguish and said, "You're not alone"? And we're indebted to God for . . . everything.

They were all generous to us before we even knew we were in need. In fact, before we even were. And their generosity—even though it was offered with no strings from them—sets up an inescapable obligation within us, provided of course we want to be men and women of honor.

That's bad enough. But it gets worse. Over and above taking life—and all that gift invites us to—for granted, we can't help but gripe that the gift wasn't more . . . unrestricted, more bountiful, less selective in distributing its specialties. "She got wealthier, more educated parents than I did; He got a better set of genes. Look at those muscles. They never have the troubles I do." We spend so much time griping about the accommodations, we never realize how childish it is, sulking because it's someone else's birthday party we were invited to, not our own.

A while ago, I was walking around the campus, just hangin' out with Jesus awhile, when I ran into a young man I'd taught two years before. He said, "You know, I've been meaning to stop around and see you. I've been thinking for a long time that you were the meanest, toughest, most relentless teacher I ever had . . . . And I never thanked you."

Well, I walked away six inches off the ground! For a teacher, gratitude's about as rare as snow in the Sahara. I imagine parents find the same rarity. You just go on, doling out, absorbing the resentment, clinging to the hope that one day Helen Keller's going to understand. You don't do it in order to be thanked. Just because . . . well, you can't help it. It's love.

And yet, paradoxically, a teacher or parent does want to be thanked. Not just because it keeps you going—though God knows it does that. But for the sake of the person you helped, so that they're not the kind of person who takes kindness—even cruel kindness—for granted. So that they become a person ennobled by gratitude.

Surely there's someone you've taken for granted, whom you've never really thanked—even though that person is truly precious to you. Think of that person. The big sister who taught you how to dance, the brother who taught you how to ride a bike, the friend who's absorbed your anger and your frustration and your tears. Maybe the grammar school nun who held your head while you were sick. Maybe the crusty coach who kept nagging you till you did what you thought you couldn't possibly do. It could even be someone who actually gave you very good advice that you ignored—and now see was the right choice.

Even if that gift giver doesn't expect it, think of the difference it will make in you. That uplift of the soul that is joy.

We're so incredibly spoiled. The very poorest kid

in my classes, the kid on third-generation welfare, is luckier than 95 percent of the other kids his age in the whole world. Half the people in the world go to bed hungry, 70 percent can't read, 80 percent are in substandard housing. If you have coins jingling in your pocket, you're rich. If your dinner tonight will be different from last night's, you're breathlessly blessed. The crucial question is whether we're also breathlessly grateful. When I say that, most kids I teach haven't the slightest notion what I'm talking about—even the ones who do service in soup kitchens.

See what I mean? Gratitude makes you very uncomfortable.

What can get rid of it? Just a few lines on a piece of notepaper and the price of a stamp.

Also there's another way. The word "Eucharist" means thanksgiving—not just for good health or material prosperity or lack of tragedy at the moment, but thanks just for the challenge of being born and then for being called to be sons and daughters of the Most High. Can we feel grateful to be entrusted with being the salt of the earth . . . the light set on a lampstand . . . the welcoming hands of the promiscuous Christ? You can't feel thankful if you're spoiled, if you take it all for granted. Who's grateful for peristalsis, respiration, binocular vision? How often do we feel a surge of blessedness when we ponder our spouses, our kids, our friends? As Chesterton says, people sometimes ask whom to thank for the presents in their stockings Christmas morning. But they rarely think to thank someone for putting legs into the stockings they put on every day.

On the one hand, we've been pretty spoiled with more than anyone needs of the world's goods, and on the other, we've been pretty impoverished of the exhilaration of the gospel's invitation to stand up and be counted—to write a letter to the editor, to tell someone on the parish council that the homilies are a test of our faith, to sit with the one who always sits alone in the cafeteria? *Noblesse oblige.*

Again, when you feel shortchanged by life, sit down with a piece of paper and list all the things you love: mountains at sunrise, star-strewn summer nights. It'll take quite a while, I'm pretty sure. When you're finished, try to thank God for inviting you into all that.

It won't enrich God very much, but it'll sure enrich you.

i thank You God for most this amazing day.

—e. e. cummings

39

Six Habits of Highly Grateful People

Jeremy Adam Smith

I'm terrible at gratitude.

How bad am I? I'm so bad at gratitude that most days, I don't notice the sunlight on the leaves of the Berkeley oaks as I ride my bike down the street. I forget to be thankful for the guy who hand-brews that delicious cup of coffee I drink mid-way through every weekday morning. I don't even know the dude's name!

I usually take for granted that I have legs to walk on, eyes to see with, arms I can use to hug my son. I forget my son! Well, I don't actually forget about him, at least as a physical presence; I generally remember to pick him up from school and feed him dinner. But as I face the quotidian slings and arrows of parenthood, I forget all the time how much he's changed my life for the better.

Gratitude (and its sibling, appreciation) is the mental tool we use to remind ourselves of the good stuff. It's a lens that helps us to see the things that don't make it onto our lists of problems to be solved. It's a spotlight that we shine on the people who give us the good things in life. It's a bright red paintbrush we apply to otherwise-invisible blessings, like clean streets or health or enough food to eat.

Gratitude doesn't make problems and threats disappear. We can lose jobs, we can be attacked on the street, we can get sick. I've experienced all of those things. I remember those harrowing times at unexpected moments: My heart beats faster, my throat constricts. My body wants to hit something or run away, one or the other. But there's nothing to hit, nowhere to run. The threats are indeed real, but at that moment, they exist only in memory or imagination. I am the threat; it is me who is wearing myself out with worry.

That's when I need to turn on the gratitude. If I do that enough, suggests the psychological research, gratitude might just become a habit. What will that mean for me? It means, says the research, that I increase my chances of psychologically surviving hard times, that I stand a chance to be happier in the good times. I'm not ignoring the threats; I'm appreciating the resources and people that might help me face those threats.

If you're already one of those highly grateful people, stop reading this essay—you don't need it. Instead you should read Amie Gordon's "Five Ways Giving Thanks Can Backfire." But if you're more like me, then here are some tips for how you and I can become one of those fantastically grateful people.

1. Once in a while, they think about death and loss

Didn't see that one coming, did you? I'm not just being perverse—contemplating endings really does make you more grateful for the life you currently have, according to several studies.

For example, when Araceli Friasa and colleagues asked people to visualize their own deaths, their gratitude measurably increased. Similarly, when Minkyung Koo and colleagues asked people to envision the sudden disappearance of their romantic partners from their lives, they became more grateful to their partners. The same goes for imagining that some positive event, like a job promotion, never happened.

This isn't just theoretical: When you find yourself

taking a good thing for granted, try giving it up for a little while. Researchers Jordi Quoidbach and Elizabeth Dunn had 55 people eat a piece of chocolate—and then the researchers told some of those people to resist chocolate for a week and others to binge on chocolate if they wanted. They left a third group to their own devices.

Guess who ended up happiest, according to self-reports? The people who abstained from chocolate. And who were the least happy? The people who binged. That's the power of gratitude!

2. *They take the time to smell the roses*

And they also smell the coffee, the bread baking in the oven, the aroma of a new car—whatever gives them pleasure.

Loyola University psychologist Fred Bryant finds that savoring positive experiences makes them stickier in your brain, and increases their benefits to your psyche—and the key, he argues, is expressing gratitude for the experience. That's one of the ways appreciation and gratitude go hand in hand.

You might also consider adding some little ritual to how you experience the pleasures of the body: A study published this year in *Psychological Science* finds that rituals like prayer or even just shaking a sugar packet "make people pay more attention to food, and paying attention makes food taste better," as Emily Nauman reports in her *Greater Good* article about the research.

This brand of mindfulness makes intuitive sense— but how does it work with the first habit above?

Well, we humans are astoundingly adaptive creatures, and we will adapt even to the good things. When we do, their subjective value starts to drop; we start to take them for granted. That's the point at which we might give them up for a while—be it chocolate, sex, or even something like sunlight—and then take the time to really savor them when we allow them back into our lives.

That goes for people, too, and that goes back to the first habit: If you're taking someone for granted, take a step back—and imagine your life without them. Then try savoring their presence, just like you would a rose. Or a new car. Whatever! The point is, absence may just make the heart grow grateful.

3. They take the good things as gifts, not birthrights

What's the opposite of gratitude? Entitlement— the attitude that people owe you something just because you're so very special.

"In all its manifestations, a preoccupation with the

self can cause us to forget our benefits and our benefactors or to feel that we are owed things from others
and therefore have no reason to feel thankful," writes
Robert Emmons, co-director of the GGSC's Gratitude project. "Counting blessings will be ineffective
because grievances will always outnumber gifts."

The antidote to entitlement, argues Emmons, is to
see that we did not create ourselves—we were created,
if not by evolution, then by God; or if not by God,
then by our parents. Likewise, we are never truly self-
sufficient. Humans need other people to grow our
food and heal our injuries; we need love, and for that
we need family, partners, friends, and pets.

"Seeing with grateful eyes requires that we see
the web of interconnection in which we alternate between being givers and receivers," writes Emmons.
"The humble person says that life is a gift to be grateful for, not a right to be claimed."

4. They're grateful to people, not just things

At the start of this piece, I mentioned gratitude for
sunlight and trees. That's great for me—and it may
have good effects, like leading me to think about my
impact on the environment—but the trees just don't
care. Likewise, the sun doesn't know I exist; that big
ball of flaming gas isn't even aware of its own exis-

tence, as far as we know. My gratitude doesn't make it burn any brighter.

That's not true of people—people will glow in gratitude. Saying thanks to my son might make him happier and it can strengthen our emotional bond. Thanking the guy who makes my coffee can strengthen social bonds—in part by deepening our understanding of how we're interconnected with other people.

My colleague Emiliana Simon-Thomas, the GGSC's science director and another co-director of our Expanding Gratitude project, puts it this way: "Experiences that heighten meaningful connections with others—like noticing how another person has helped you, acknowledging the effort it took, and savoring how you benefitted from it—engage biological systems for trust and affection, alongside circuits for pleasure and reward. This provides a synergistic and enduring boost to the positive experience. Saying 'thank you' to a person, your brain registers that something good has happened and that you are more richly enmeshed in a meaningful social community."

5. They mention the pancakes

Grateful people are habitually specific. They don't say, "I love you because you're just so wonderfully wonderful, you!" Instead, the really skilled grateful person will say: "I love you for the pancakes you make when you see I'm hungry and the way you massage my feet after work even when you're really tired and how you give me hugs when I'm sad so that I'll feel better!"

The reason for this is pretty simple: It makes the expression of gratitude feel more authentic, for it reveals that the thanker was genuinely paying attention and isn't just going through the motions. The richest thank yous will acknowledge intentions ("the pancakes you make when you see I'm hungry") and costs ("you massage my feet after work even when you're really tired"), and they'll describe the value of benefits received ("you give me hugs when I'm sad so that I'll feel better").

When Amie Gordon and colleagues studied gratitude in couples, they found that spouses signal grateful feelings through more caring and attentive behavior. They ask clarifying questions; they respond to trouble with hugs and to good news with smiles. "These gestures," Gordon writes, "can have profound effects: Participants who were better listeners during those conversations in the lab had partners who reported feeling more appreciated by them."

Remember: Gratitude thrives on specificity!

6. *They thank outside the box*

But let's get real: Pancakes, massages, hugs? Boring! Most of my examples so far are easy and clichéd. But here's who the really tough-minded grateful person thanks: the boyfriend who dumped her, the homeless person who asked for change, the boss who laid him off.

We're graduating from Basic to Advanced Gratitude, so pay attention. And since I myself am still working on Basic, I'll turn once again to Dr. Emmons for guidance: "It's easy to feel grateful for the good things. No one 'feels' grateful that he or she has lost a job or a home or good health or has taken a devastating hit on his or her retirement portfolio."

In such moments, he says, gratitude becomes a critical cognitive process—a way of thinking about the world that can help us turn disaster into a stepping stone. If we're willing and able to look, he argues, we can find a reason to feel grateful even to people who have harmed us. We can thank that boyfriend for being brave enough to end a relationship that wasn't working; the homeless person for reminding us of our advantages and vulnerability; the boss, for forcing us to face new challenges.

"Life is suffering. No amount of positive thinking exercises will change this truth," writes Emmons in his Greater Good article "How Gratitude Can Help You Through Hard Times." He continues: "So telling people simply to buck up, count their blessings, and remember how much they still have to be grateful for can certainly do much harm. Processing a life experience through a grateful lens does not mean denying negativity. It is not a form of superficial happiology. Instead, it means realizing the power you have to transform an obstacle into an opportunity. It means reframing a loss into a potential gain, recasting negativity into positive channels for gratitude." That's what truly, fantastically grateful people do. Can you?

40

A Tangerine Party

Thich Nhat Hanh

Yesterday, in our retreat, we had a tangerine party. Everyone was offered one tangerine. We put the tangerine on the palm of our hand and looked at it, breathing in a way that the tangerine became real. Most of the time when we eat a tangerine, we do not look at it. We think about many other things. To look at a tangerine is to see the blossom forming into the fruit, to see the sunshine and the rain. The tangerine in our palm is the wonderful presence of life. We are able to really see that tangerine and smell its blossom and the warm, moist earth. As the tangerine becomes real, we become real. Life in that moment becomes real.

Mindfully we began to peel our tangerine and smell its fragrance. We carefully took each section of the tangerine and put it on our tongue, and we could feel that it was a real tangerine. We ate each section of the tangerine in perfect mindfulness until we finished the entire fruit. Eating a tangerine in this way is very important, because both the tangerine and the eater of the tangerine become real. This, too, is the basic work for peace.

In Buddhist meditation we do not struggle for the kind of enlightenment that will happen five or ten years from now. We practice so that each moment of our life becomes real life. And, therefore, when we meditate, we sit for sitting; we don't sit for something else. If we sit for twenty minutes, these twenty minutes should bring us joy, life. If we practice walking meditation, we walk just for walking, not to arrive. We have to be alive with each step, and if we are, each step brings real life back to us. The same kind of mindfulness can be practiced when we eat breakfast, or when we hold a child in our arms. Hugging is a Western custom, but we from the East would like to contribute the practice of conscious breathing to it. When you hold a child in your arms, or hug your mother, or your husband, or your friend, breathe in and out three times and your happiness will be multiplied by at least tenfold. And when you look at someone, really look at them with mindfulness, and practice conscious breathing.

At the beginning of each meal, I recommend that you look at your plate and silently recite, "My plate is empty now, but I know that it is going to be filled with delicious food in just a moment." While waiting to be served or to serve yourself, I suggest you breathe three times and look at it even more deeply. "At this very moment many, many people around the world are also holding a plate, but their plate is going to be empty for a long time." Forty thousand children die each day because of the lack of food. Children alone. We can be very happy to have such wonderful food, but we also suffer because we are capable of seeing. But when we see in this way, it makes us sane, because the way in front of us is clear—the way to live so that we can make peace with ourselves and with the world. When we see the good and the bad, the wondrous and the deep suffering, we have to live in a way that we can make peace between ourselves and the world. Understanding is the fruit of meditation. Understanding is the basis of everything.

Each breath we take, each step we make, each smile we realize, is a positive contribution to peace, a necessary step in the direction of peace for the world. In the light of interbeing, peace and happiness in your daily life means peace and happiness in the world.

Thank You

To be grateful is to recognize the Love of God in everything He has given us—and He has given us everything. Every breath we draw is a gift of His love, every moment of existence is a grace, for it brings with it immense graces from Him. Gratitude therefore takes nothing for granted, is never unresponsive, is constantly awakening to new wonder and to praise of the goodness of God. For the grateful person knows that God is good, not by hearsay but by experience. And that is what makes all the difference.

—THOMAS MERTON

41

The Buddha Who Lives in Our Backyard

Michael Leach

"You must go on, I can't go on, I'll go on."
—WAITING FOR GODOT

We planted a cherry tree and placed a Buddha on top of some rocks beneath it, outside the big window by our kitchen table so we can look out and focus on peace. True story: The Buddha was a prince named Siddhartha Gautama who left his palace in India at age twenty-nine to wander the world in search of the meaning of life. He was profoundly moved by all the suffering he saw. One day he sat under a bodhi tree and prayed to God for understanding. He realized that suffering is inevitable, that his response must be loving kindness, and that the purpose of life is compassion. He became the Buddha (an enlightened presence) and felt peace, even as petals from the tree fell around him like tears.

Early this morning, Vickie and I stand by the window. On the window sill, a teeny plastic flower pot with a white daisy and two yellow butterflies sits. When the sun rises higher and puts out all the darkness, the flower will wave and the butterflies dance. The toy gets its energy from light. Vickie and I look out at the Buddha sitting atop the gray stones. "Good morning, Mr. Buddha," I say. Then like George Burns to Gracie Allen: "Say 'good morning' to Mr. Buddha, sweetheart."

"Good morning . . . Mistuh . . . Buddha."

The words don't come easy. Vickie suffered two brain seizures recently. She was diagnosed with Alzheimer's ten years ago. The door in her brain to a thesaurus of words has been closing faster. Vickie's neurologist gave her an anti-seizure medicine that has doused her delight like a gloved hand snuffs out a candle. I will call her doctor later today and say: "What's worse, to never again have a seizure but live out your life as a paranoid schizophrenic or live a little shorter but in peace?"

We sit at the kitchen table and share a banana. "I

want to put a Mary in your little garden next to the patio," I say. "What do you think?"

"Good."

"There's a Mary Southard sculpture called Our Lady of the Garden. I showed it to you yesterday. It's whiter than snow and real peaceful."

"What?"

"Mary Southard. She's a sister, an artist, an old friend."

The white sculpture of the Blessed Mother will be perfect. Vickie has tended her little garden since we moved into this house 30 years ago. I always say, "If you die first, I'll bury your ashes in your garden. A fountain will come forth and all the people who live here for years to come will drink from your joy."

"What if you die first?"

"Then you'll bury me first. A desert will take over, but when you die, our boys will put your ashes next to mine and a spring will bubble up and a fountain even more wondrous than the one with your ashes alone."

It's time to take Vickie to the adult day care center. It's a lovely place overlooking a waterfall where the Mianus River flows into Long Island Sound. Six aides, along with a nurse, a social worker and a program coordinator look after about 50 women and men with Alzheimer's or other incapacities or just need company from 9 to 4. They socialize, have visits from schoolchildren, pets from the animal shelter, mini-concerts from local artists, and if they can, take field trips to the beach or museum. It gives caregivers a chance to do their work or just get a break. I take Vickie twice a week and am thinking of making it three. She likes it there and Vickie, always the helper, looks after Joyce, who is about her age and also forgetful.

She doesn't want to go today. I ask her to do it for me.

We get in the car, back out and turn into the driveway of the house next door to pick up Rob. Rob is 53 years old and walks with a walker because his muscles are weak and his legs move in directions he doesn't want them to go. His dad is older than I am and recovering from a heart attack. I told Terri, his wife, that we would take Rob to the day center because he goes there too and she has her hands full.

Rob bends over, one hand on the walker, to pick up a stray leaf on the driveway and place it on the lawn. "Rob," says Terri, "don't do that. You'll just fall." Rob does fall a lot. And gets up. And goes on. He, too, has difficulty communicating, but his eyes understand suffering in others and you can tell he cares about them.

I call the doctor later in the morning, and she changes the medicine to something with fewer side effects. She says the effects of the first should be gone by tomorrow afternoon. I try to write my column for Soul Seeing, but nothing comes. I pick up Vickie and Rob at 3:30. "How was your day?" I ask her. "Horrible," she says.

We sit at the kitchen table and share a brownie. I can't make her laugh. Helping Vickie dress, bathe, all that, is nothing. Not making her laugh kills. I take her hand and we go to the window and look at the Buddha who lives in our backyard. A gopher sips at the water in the birdbath beneath him. "Sweetheart," I say, "let's ask Mr. Buddha what we need to know right now. OK?"

"OK."

I pray in my heart to God for a miracle.

After a few moments, I ask Vickie, "Did Mr. Buddha tell you anything?"

She smiles at me. "Thank you."

The dandelion and the butterflies dance before darkness falls. Tomorrow is another day, but for now, Mr. Buddha has moved inside.

42

Attitude of Gratitude

Helen Grace Lescheid

*"Give thanks in all circumstances, for this is
God's will for you in Christ Jesus"*
—1 Thessalonians 5:18

Everyone needs a mentor, a person who models for
you the Christian walk. A person you look up to and
say, "I'd like to be like her when I'm that age."

Anna is this person for me. At 81 Anna lives alone
in a small one bedroom apartment in a Salvation
Army Senior independent living complex. Her husband died six years ago. Because she's experiencing
severe memory loss, Anna has had to give up driving
her car.

But Anna has not a shred of self-pity. Her face
was radiant as she told me, "Glen and I had almost
twenty-five years together." Then she laughed,

"Counting our courting days, it was twenty-five years. His son, Ron, is so good to me. He looks after all my affairs."

To the loss of her car she said, "Just think how much money I'm saving by not driving a car." Then she added, "Besides, walking to the mall does me good. I buy my groceries at *Save-On-Foods*, then haul them home in my little cart. And when I can't walk anymore, I'll get a scooter." She was exuberant that the mall also had a vet office, a bank, a beauty salon and several restaurants. "Everything I need is right here," she said.

To memory loss she quipped, "Good thing I'm methodical and I write everything down. That helps. And I'm taking medication against Alzheimer's." As we talked about the future she expressed absolutely no fear, only a joyous expectancy of heaven.

When I showed her a photo I'd taken of her on my digital camera, she smiled, "Yes, that's me." No disparaging remarks about her looks (like I would have made) not even in jest. As far as Anna was concerned life was good and she was making the best of it.

Anna took me out for lunch at a Chinese restaurant within walking distance to her home. She insisted on paying for the meal. "Then let me give the tip," I said. She agreed and I left a generous tip on the table. Minutes later I heard her say to the girl at the till, "Please add the tip to the bill." Just like Anna, I thought, to leave a double blessing.

43

Interfaith Thanksgiving
A Story of Gratitude and
Self-Balancing Acts

Mike Ghouse

Expression of gratitude is the ultimate balancing act in everyone's life. We know whom we receive the good from and offer our gratitude. The absence of a simple thank you creates an imbalance in the relationship and spiritual energy, while a simple thank you restores it.

I am pleased to share my personal story and a few small things you can do to regain your sense of composure and balance.

First, we need to be considerate to those who did not have a good childhood, youth, adulthood or retirement. Let's be kind to those who are struggling to take care of themselves, and fighting for a square meal for their families. The least we can do for them is to let them know that we care.

Second, we need to awaken our mentor, be it Zarathustra, Moses, Krishna, Buddha, Mahavira, Jesus, Muhammad, Tao, Confucius, Nanak, Bahaullah, Gandhi, MLK or whomever we hold dearly. We need to emulate them for at least for the day as an experiment, ready to embrace every one with a caring attitude.

Finally, let's make a list of people who have helped us shape our lives. We should not lose enthusiasm due to a large number of people we have to thank. We can do it by carrying a piece of paper, and writing down the names as they pop in the mind. Even if we don't call everyone on the list, we have already said our thanks by thinking about the individual and writing his or her name down. When we express our gratitude to the person who has made a difference in our life, it brings a ton of relief. It's ours to keep.

The Unforgettable Story of Appaiah

It was a Sunday ritual for me to sit and take care of the poor. A line of the needy people would pass in front of my house, and since I was the oldest in the family, my father had assigned me the task of doling out the alms to the individuals when they passed by our door. I have seen lepers, people who cannot see, hear or talk, and people with missing body parts.

I was fascinated by one such person. He did not have arms and limbs from the base of the body; he was just a torso with a head. He wrapped his body with a tube (in those days car tires were inlaid with rubber tubes to hold the air) of a car tire, and would slide inch by inch on his back from door to door . . . His shoulder and rear part would move in tandem similar to a snake.

It was beyond me to understand Appaiah. I often wondered, what is there for him in life? The fourteen year old in me was full of ambition, and was looking forward to getting my education, finding work, getting married, having a house and kids. I was a typical teenager loaded with testosterone and could not imagine life beyond that.

Why does he not commit suicide? What is there for him to look forward to? One day, I asked him. "Appaiah, you don't have relatives, can't do anything, don't have a place to live, and can't wear clothes . . . why do you want to live?"

He turned around and took a deep breath and looked at me. He made an effort to move, but could not, and said, "Son, I look forward to every morning to see the blue sky or see the rain and smell the earth. I taste the good food people give me. I am thankful to God for giving me these eyes to see the beauty of his creation." I was watching him; he did not have the arms to point to his eyes. He then asked me, "Isn't there so much to be thankful for? Live for?"

He was poetic, philosophical and pragmatic. He shattered my bias to smithereens. Here I was thinking, what does this guy know?

I was rendered speechless. Here is a man with nothing to hope for, yet he is not complaining. Instead, he is appreciating what he has, which is nothing. That was quite an influencing experience in my life to treat others as I would want to be treated (Bible).

Just that morning, I heard my dad's favorite verse from Quran: "Then which of the favors of your Lord will ye deny?" (55:16). Now, when hopelessness hits me, I go to the Scriptures. I have found solace in opening Bhagavad Gita, Bible, Guru Granth Saheb, Dale Carnegie's book, Kitáb-i-Aqdas or simply read Sura Rahman, chapter 55 in Quran, to uplift my spirits. We have to be grateful for whatever we have and express it to the unknown giver, a true thanksgiving.

You can only feel the joy when you say a big or a small thank you to the ones who have helped you along the way, whether it is materially, spiritually or professionally.

A simple thank you will do a lot of good to us, and our relationships. Most people say thanks without fail, those who miss out on a few things; we have an opportunity to reflect on this on Thanksgiving Day.

If you don't believe in God, that is fine; it is still a release when you say thanks to the invisible good that came to you un-asked.

Life Is a Self-Balancing Act

Life is a self-balancing act; everything we do and say is spiritual as well as a real life transaction that moves the needle from balance to imbalance, and back to balance.

The mechanism is built around forgiveness, repentance, service and gratitude. These values are a product of co-existence and inculcated through religious teachings; however, the atheists would also achieve the same without invoking God.

The accountant chants, for every debit there is a credit; the physicist has proved that for every action there is an equal and opposite reaction, and the doctor declares that blood lost from the body of an individual must be replenished with an equal amount of blood to sustain life.

As a spiritualist I say, for every wrong we do, an equal amount of energy is drained from us, and for every good we do, energy is recouped. We are constantly receiving and giving energy. Intake and output must be equal to have a healthy life, or else we are thrown off balance.

For every hurt we hurl on others, an equal amount of burden gets dumped on us, and until we say sorry and repent genuinely, the energy balance within us deteriorates. The transaction remains incomplete.

Where Is Happiness?

If you are single or empty nesters with nowhere to go, call up the Salvation Army, a hospital or a homeless shelter and volunteer your services. There is a joy in serving others.

As the Jewish Scriptures say, *Ve'ahavta la'ger*—you must love the stranger for that guaranteed happiness. Jesus reached out to the ones who were abandoned by the society. Prophet Muhammad said the least you can give to others is hope and a smile. The Hindu Scriptures guide you to treat the whole world as one family. Buddha, the learned one, taught the joys of living for others. The Sikh faith is indeed founded on the principle of caring for humanity. The Jains and Baha'i believe our joy comes from taking care of others. The Native Americans and Wicca believe we have to take care of what we see around us and preserve it for the next seven generations. With malice toward none is a good advice from Mahatma Lincoln to follow.

Happy Thanksgiving

When you express your gratitude to the persons who have made a difference in your life, it brings a ton of relief to you. Make an effort and enjoy the peace of mind that comes with it. May you be blessed to be a blessing to others. Amen!

44

Let Us Be Grateful

Mother Mary Joseph Rogers, MM

We are all familiar with the story of the lepers who came before Our Lord asking Him to heal them. We are all familiar with the dreadful condition of a person stricken with leprosy. We know he is an outcast from society and we can realize the boon they were asking of Our Lord was a priceless one. In His mercy, He healed all of them. They went on their way rejoicing, and showed themselves to the priests and were declared cleansed, but only one came back to give thanks.

Certainly it is not without a purpose, without a special lesson for us, that this particular miracle is recorded in the Scriptures. Only one of ten returned to give thanks to God for a priceless gift. It makes us realize how rare gratitude is. It makes us realize how selfish most of the world is, how self-centered . . . It is good for us to examine ourselves on this point, and ask ourselves whether or not gratitude is characteristic of us. I think most of us will find that it is a virtue we need seriously to cultivate.

In each of us there are many things for which we should be grateful. God has created the world about us, full of beauties, filled with all the things we need to sustain life. We have the day in which to work and the night in which rest comes to us. We have the fruits of the earth, animal life to feed and nourish us, various materials from which our clothing and other necessities of life come to us, and most of these things we simply take for granted. We think nothing about them and if sometimes our hearts are lifted on high, when we are conscious of something unusually beautiful about us, it is too often an appreciation of that beauty with little or no thought of a prayer of gratitude to God Who gave it to us.

Most of us, individually, can look back upon a family life in which there was everything for which to be thankful. The tender love of parents, love of brothers and sisters. We look back upon the unselfishness and sacrifice of our parents—think of the things they denied themselves that we might have things which they did not have in their youth—and most of us, again, must realize that we took much, if not most, of this as something due to us, or, if we did not think of it as selfishly as that, we took it simply for granted and the natural expression of parental love . . .

Let us think often of the gospel story of the lepers. It was told not to emphasize the boundless mercy of Christ and the Son of God; it was told, apparently, simply to impress on us how rare is gratitude, and yet it should be a common virtue . . . Let us, therefore, look into our souls today, let us express our gratitude along the various lines of which we have been thinking. Are we grateful to God for His particular gifts, for His general gifts? Are we grateful to our parents, brothers and sisters and benefactors? Are we grateful to our friends? It should not satisfy us simply to say, "I am grateful, I owe thanks," the great point is this: Is our gratefulness, our gratitude an active thing?

In our life, gratitude can be expressed in a thousand ways, but chiefly apart from prayer, in expressions by word and kind deeds the gratitude we owe to one another. Now, if we find that we are particularly lacking in this virtue, and I fear some of us are, let us make a very strong resolution to be watchful over ourselves.Let us resolve to make concrete the feelings of gratitude which must well up in our hearts, so that we may not be like the lepers, of whom Christ asked: "Where are the others, were they not also cured?"

45

Praying as a Parent

Mary Beth Werdel

I was at Sunday Mass with my son, Peter, who was almost six years old. He was quiet and focused intensely on his color-by-number sheet. I was aware I was feeling grateful that Peter was able to be calmly present in church without being disruptive. Lately, Peter has become aware that if he screams certain phrases in a loud voice, his father will take him out of Mass. His latest phrases include: "I want to go home," "Can I have a donut?" or the most theologically concerning phrase of all, "I don't believe this anyway!" As I noted his contentment, so too I observed my own. I could hear the lectors and the priest; I could take part in the communal prayer; I was present in the Mass. I found myself thinking, "Isn't this how church was meant to be?"

The Strength of Colors

I was grateful for Peter's coloring, an activity he refused to engage in until recently, which puzzled me for many years. I had watched other children sit contentedly with their crayons. Not Peter. An occupational therapist who worked with him explained that Peter had an immature pencil grasp. Peter's brain had difficulties knowing where to place his fingers. He didn't realize innately how hard or soft to push to make the crayon "work." Peter could read, count by 5s, 10s and even 12s. But coloring, the task that seemed easiest for his peers, which allowed him to be in relationship with them, was a monumental struggle.

When Peter was two years old, a psychologist told me that he met the criteria for autism. He also told me that Peter had a superior I.Q. Somehow the former statement always seemed to rattle in my mind and heart a bit louder and longer than the latter. I struggled to hear any blessing. In a sign of resignation, sometime along the way, I stopped carrying crayons in my purse and started praying Peter would miraculously behave in church.

One day, while Peter was with his grandmother, he came across a color-by-number. Something inside him clicked; he started coloring. With regular coloring there are no rules or order. Peter thrives on rules. He feels safe. A lack of rules causes anxiety. When it comes to coloring, it leads at best to giving up. With the color-by-number, Peter wanted to follow the coloring rule so intensely that he held the crayon any way he could. With time he started to hold it differently, the way his therapist had so many times tried to teach him. Ever so proudly, he came to me one day exclaiming, "Mommy my hand hurts from all the coloring. It is getting stronger!"

Then it got even better.

As Peter calmly colored in the pew, he began participating in Mass. He was even engaged in the homily as he responded to me so sweetly in a moment of great connection: "Mommy, the priest said Moses. Moses is from my Bible." Later in the Mass, Peter started to sing. That Sunday, instead of screaming, he was singing "Hosanna" loudly. He was singing with heart and joy. His joy brought my joy; my joy in return encouraged his.

That was until the Hosanna ended and Peter didn't. My first instinct was to stop him, thinking about how he may be bothering fellow churchgoers and how his continued song represented my inadequacy as a parent. Instead of immediately asking

Peter to stop singing, I detached myself from feelings of guilt and embarrassment, and as my mentor, psychologist and author Robert Wicks reminds me so often to do, I "leaned back" and looked at what was happening around me with a quiet mind and an open heart.

Learning to Lean Back

Peter was in Mass on a Sunday morning. Peter was singing a beautiful prayer. People around him were smiling, some laughing. When I put my need for Peter's compliance and my commitment to order aside, I noticed I was feeling gratitude for Peter's continued growth and development, for the experience of joy that he and I both seemed filled with in this moment, and for our shared connection to something greater than ourselves. When I leaned back I questioned: What would I be teaching Peter by asking him to stop? What would he remember of my parenting in the moments, days and years to come when we forget the words but remember the feelings people create for us? So, I did what I have found can sometimes be the most profoundly difficult yet important stance to take as a parent. I held the space for Peter to be Peter; I allowed him to sing.

When he eventually stopped, instead of telling

him he was not following the order of Mass or using some phrase that would convey the idea that his six-year-old presence was a nuisance to others, I leaned close to him, gave him a kiss and told him I loved him very much. He smiled as he continued coloring.

If I had not leaned back in the moment, I wonder what I would have really asked of him? What lesson would I have unknowingly encouraged or discouraged? Sometimes, in an effort to make sure Peter is not bothering other people, I forget that Peter prays too, that he has a right to sing and that it is a sign of engagement that he asks questions.

When I lean back, I am able to respond rather than react. I am able to create space to honor curiosity and engagement with the experience. When I lean back, I can be a more effective parent. I notice that I want my children to be respectful, to know how to have self-control and to be able to quiet their minds and bodies—but quiet not as an end in itself but as a means to a relationship with the sacred. My goal is to help Peter create space in his heart so that he can be filled with grace and peace, perspective and love, curiosity and awe; so that as an adult he may be just as he is now as a child, full of wonder before God.

Matthew 18:3 reads, "Truly, I say to you, unless

you turn and become like children, you will never enter the kingdom of heaven." There are days when I wonder exactly which children this verse is speaking about, because surely it is not the three I bring to church. But on days like this Sunday morning, I see that of course it is my children it applies to, and of course it is I.

When I lean back I notice that parenting Peter allows me access to deep gratitude. Peter is continually surprised anew by his joy that results from overcoming each struggle, and so then I find myself continually grateful anew. While my body is growing old, Peter helps me to keep my heart open and my eyes young so that I may remain grateful, so that I may know God and so that Peter and I may become more whole together.

Sometimes I find myself wishing that parenting could be more like a color-by-number than the abstract experience that is its nature. When I feel centered and empty my heart before God, I can recognize that maybe the goal is not joy. Rather, joy is the byproduct of gratitude. If my prayers focus on a desire to be more grateful, then the very crayons I use as a parent may look more vibrant, the ways I stay in the lines or don't stay in the lines may look more beautiful. And, just maybe, the process of my children and I becoming us, which never ends, may feel more wondrous and right.

There is so much to pray for when one is a parent. But that which is in my control and has the ability to color my perspective of life experiences is my capacity to look for gratitude: in the purpose I have as a mother; the practice I am given seemingly every second of the day to become a mother; the God whom I love and who loved me first, who gave me this responsibility; and the lives that I am allowed to nurture, which in turn nurture me. My prayers are that one day I may learn to maintain a perspective in parenting so that I may feel not waves of appreciation, but that in each moment of parenting, I may feel ever blessed.

46

Awake, Aware, and Alert

David Steindl-Rast

Three Steps in the Process of Living a Life of Gratefulness

An act of gratitude is a living whole. To superimpose on its organic flow a mental grid like a series of "steps" will always be somewhat arbitrary. And yet, for the sake of practice, such a delineation can be helpful. In any process, we can distinguish a beginning, a middle, and an end. We may use this basic three-step grid for the practice of gratitude: What happens at the start, in the middle, and at the end, when we experience gratitude? What fails to happen when we are not grateful? Before going to bed, I glance back over the day and ask myself: Did I stop and allow myself to be surprised? Or, did I trudge on in a daze? To be awake, aware, and alert are the beginning, middle, and end of gratitude. This gives us the clue to what the three basic steps of practicing gratitude must be.

Step One: Wake Up

To begin with, we never start to be grateful unless we wake up. Wake up to what? To surprise. As long as nothing surprises us, we walk through life in a daze. We need to practice waking up to surprise. I suggest using this simple question as a kind of alarm clock: "Isn't this surprising?" "Yes, indeed!" will be the correct answer, no matter when and where and under what circumstances you ask this question. After all, isn't it surprising that there is anything at all, rather than nothing? Ask yourself at least twice a day, "Isn't this surprising?" and you will soon be more awake to the surprising world in which we live.

Surprise may provide a jolt, enough to wake us up and to stop taking everything for granted. But we may not at all like that surprise. "How can I be grateful for something like this?" we may howl in the midst of a sudden calamity. And why? Because we are not aware of the real gift in this given situation: opportunity.

Step Two: Be Aware of Opportunities

There is a simple question that helps me to practice the second step of gratitude: "What's my opportunity here?" You will find that most of the time, the opportunity that a given moment offers you is an opportunity to enjoy—to enjoy sounds, smells, tastes, texture, colors, and, with still deeper joy, friendliness, kindness, patience, faithfulness, honesty, and all those gifts that soften the soil of our heart like warm spring rain. The more we practice awareness of the countless opportunities to simply enjoy, the easier it becomes to recognize difficult or painful experiences as opportunities, as gifts.

But while awareness of opportunities inherent in life events and circumstances is the core of gratefulness, awareness alone is not enough. What good is it to be aware of an opportunity, unless we avail ourselves of it? How grateful we are shows itself by the alertness with which we respond to the opportunity.

Step Three: Respond Alertly

Once we are in practice for being awake to surprise and being aware of the opportunity at hand, we will spontaneously be alert in our response, especially when we are offered an opportunity to enjoy something. When a sudden rain shower is no longer just an inconvenience but a surprise gift, you will spontaneously rise to the opportunity for enjoyment. You will enjoy it as much as you did in your kindergarten days, even if you are no longer trying to catch raindrops in your wide-open mouth. Only when the opportunity demands more from you than spontaneous enjoyment will you have to give yourself a bit of an extra push as part of Step Three.

The Review Process

It helps me to review my own practice of gratefulness by applying to these three basic steps the rule I learned as a boy for crossing an intersection: "Stop, look, go." Before going to bed, I glance back over the day and ask myself: Did I stop and allow myself to be surprised? Or did I trudge on in a daze? Was I too busy to wake up to surprise? And once I stopped, did I look for the opportunity of that moment? Or did I allow the circumstances to distract me from the gift within the gift? (This tends to happen when the gift's wrappings are not attractive.) And finally, was I alert enough to go after it, to avail myself fully of the opportunity offered to me?

There are times, I must admit, when stopping at night to review my day seems to be the first stop on an express train. Then I look back and realize with regret how much I missed. Not only was I less grateful on those nonstop days, I was less alive, somehow numb. Other days may be just as busy, but I do remember to stop; on those days, I even accomplish more because stopping breaks up the routine. But unless I also look, the stopping alone will not make my day a truly happy one; what difference does it make that I am not on an express train but on a local if I'm not aware of the scenery outside the windows? On some days, I even find in my nightly review that I stopped and I looked, but not with alertness. Just yesterday, I found a huge moth on the sidewalk; I did stop long enough to put it in a safe spot on the lawn, just a foot away, but I didn't crouch down to spend time with this marvelous creature. Only faintly did I remember, at night, those iridescent eyes on the grayish brown wings. My day was diminished by this failure to stay long enough with this surprise gift to deeply look at it and to savor its beauty gratefully.

My simple recipe for a joyful day is this: stop and wake up; look and be aware of what you see; then go on with all the alertness you can muster for the opportunity the moment offers. Looking back in the evening, on a day on which I made these three steps over and over, is like looking at an apple orchard heavy with fruit.

This recipe for grateful living sounds simple—because it is. But simple does not mean easy. Some of the simplest things are difficult because we have lost our childlike simplicity and have not yet found our mature one. Growth in gratitude is growth in maturity. Growth, of course, is an organic process. And so we come back to what I said at the beginning: to superimpose on the organic flow of gratitude a mental grid like a series of "steps" will remain arbitrary. When I am grateful, I am neither rushing nor slouching through my day—I'm dancing. What is true in dance class is true here too: only when you forget to think of your steps, do you truly dance.

Last Word

If the only prayer you ever say in your entire life is thank you, it will be enough.

—Meister Eckhart

Sources and Acknowledgments

1. Rowan Williams, "In the Beginning There Was Kindness," from Joan Chittister and Rowan Williams, *Uncommon Gratitude: Alleluia for All That Is.* Collegeville, MN: Liturgical Press, 2010. Copyright © 2010 by Order of Saint Benedict. Used with permission.

2. Wendell Berry, "IX.," from *Leavings: Poems.* Berkeley, CA: Counterpoint Press, 2010. Copyright © 2010 by Wendell Berry. Reprinted with permission.

3. David Brooks, "The Structure of Gratitude," *The New York Times*, July 28, 2015. Copyright © 2015 *The New York Times.* Used by permission.

4. James Martin, SJ, "Rejoice Always," from *Sick, and You Cared for Me: Homilies and Reflections for Cycle B*, Deacon Jim Knipper, ed. Princeton, NJ: Clear Faith Publishing, 2014. Reprinted by permission of the author.

5. Denise Levertov, "Gloria," from "Mass for the Day of St. Thomas Didymus, ii. Gloria," in *Candles in Babylon.* New York: New Directions Publishing, 1982. Copyright © 1982 by Denise Levertov. Reprinted by permission.

6. Patrick Manning, "The Beauty and Promise of Christian Gratitude: How Thanksgiving Can Help Us to Understand Our Deepest Desires," from *America Magazine*, November 23, 2015.

7. Jack Kornfield, "Meditation on Gratitude and Joy," from *The Art of Forgiveness, Lovingkindness, and Peace.* Copyright © 2002 by Jack Kornfield. Reprinted by permission of the author.

8. Robert Morneau, "The Color of Gratitude," from *The Color of Gratitude.* Maryknoll, NY: Orbis Books, 2009. Copyright © 2009 by Robert Morneau.

9. Henri Nouwen, "All Is Grace," from *All Is Grace*, originally published in *Weavings*, November 1992. Used by permission of the Henri Nouwen Legacy Trust.

10. Mother Mary Joseph Rogers, MM, "Love and Gratitude," excerpt from the writings of Mother Mary Joseph Rogers, 1940, Maryknoll, New York. Used by permission of the Maryknoll Sisters.

11. Joel Blunk, "Stand Up and Go; Your Faith Has Saved You," from *Hungry, and You Fed Me: Homilies for Cycle C,* Deacon Jim Knipper, ed., Princeton, NJ: Clear Faith Publishing, 2012. Reprinted by permission of the author.

12. Oliver Sacks, "My Own Life," originally published in *The New York Times*, February 19, 2015. Copyright © 2015 by Oliver Sacks, used by permission of The Wylie Agency LLC.

13. Brendan Busse, SJ, "For Your Goodness—A Prayer of Gratitude Trying Times," from *The Jesuit Post*, July 12, 2016.

14. Thich Nhat Hanh, "The Sun of Awareness," from *The Sun My Heart: Reflections on Mindfulness, Concentration and Insight.* Berkeley, CA: Parallax Press, 2006.

15. Joyce Rupp, "Fill Me at Daybreak with Gratitude," from "Thanks for Each New Day," *Inviting God In: Scriptural Reflections and Prayers Throughout the Year* (adapted). Notre Dame, IN: Ave Maria Press, 2001.

16. e. e. cummings, "I thank You God for most this amazing." Copyright © 1950, 1978, 1991 by the Trustees for the e. e. cummings Trust. Copyright © 1979 by George James Firmage, from *Complete Poems: 1904-1962* by e. e. cummings, edited by George J. Firmage. Used by permission of Liveright Publishing Corporation.

17. "Put on the New Self," Colossians 3:1-17, *New American Standard Bible* (NASB) version. Copyright © 1960, 1962, 1963, 1968, 1971, 1972, 1973, 1975, 1977, 1995 by The Lockman Foundation. Used by permission, www.Lockman.org.

18. Adam Hoffman, "What Does a Grateful Brain Look Like?," originally published in *Greater Good*, the online magazine of the Greater Good Science Center, UC Berkeley, November 16, 2015, www.greatergood.berkeley.edu.

19. "Dishwashing with Reverence," from *Wind Bell*, a publication of the San Francisco Zen Center, vol. 7, nos. 3-4, Fall 1968.

20. Frank J. Cunningham, "When Gratitude Becomes a Habit of the Heart," from *Vesper Time: Aging as a Spiritual Journey.* Maryknoll, NY: Orbis Books, 2017.

21. Anne Lamott, "Counting Our Blessings: Why We Say Grace," originally published in *Parade Magazine*, November 28, 2013. Copyright 2013 by Anne Lamott, used by permission of The Wylie Agency LLC.

22. James Martin, "Gratitude and the Spiritual Life," adapted from *The Jesuit Guide to (Almost) Everything*, 88-89 and 263-64. Copyright © 2010 by James Martin, SJ. New York: HarperCollins, 2010. Reprinted by permission of HarperCollins Publishers.

23. Helen Moore, "I Awaken Before Dawn," October 8, 2015, www.onbeing.org.

24. Joyce Rupp, "Unnoticed Prosperity," for *The Way of Gratitude: Readings for a Joyful Life.* Maryknoll, NY: Orbis Books, 2017. Used by permission of Joyce Rupp.

25. Henri Nouwen, "A Discipline," from *The Return of the Prodigal Son: A Story of Homecoming.* Copyright © 1992 by Henri J. M. Nouwen. Used by permission of Doubleday Religion, an imprint of the Crown Publishing Group, a division of Penquin Random House LLC. All rights reserved.

26. Carol Howard Merritt, "They Had Caught a Great Number of Fish and Their Nets Were Tearing," from *Hungry, and You Fed Me*, Deacon Jim Knipper, ed., Princeton, NJ: Clear Faith Publishing, 2012. Used by permission of the author.

27. Terrance W. Klein, "Glenn, the Mayor of Woodhaven: On the Importance of Gratitude in Life," from *America Magazine*, September 16, 2016.

28. Helen Phillips, MM, "A Golden Cloud." Used by permission of Sr. Helen Phillips.

29. "Thanksgiving for the Lord's Saving Goodness," Psalm 118. *New American Standard Bible* (NASB) version. Copyright © 1960, 1962, 1963, 1968, 1971, 1972, 1973, 1975, 1977, 1995 by The Lockman Foundation. Used by permission, www.Lockman.org.

30. Kelli Wheeler, "Five Inspirational Ways to Gain Greater Gratitude," from "Tips for Personal Transformation," *Maria Shriver*, November 17, 2014, www.mariashriver.com. Used by permission of Kelli Wheeler.

31. Mary Oliver, "Messenger," from *Thirst*. Boston: Beacon Press, 2004. Copyright © 2004 by Mary Oliver. Used by permission of the Charlotte Sheedy Literary Agency, Inc.

32. Dietrich Bonhoeffer, "Gratefulness: A Source of Strength," Copyright © 2015 Gratefulness.org, a Network for Grateful Living, www.gratefulness.org. Translated by Karin Murad.

33. Harijot Singh Khalsa, "Attitude of Gratitude." Used by permission of Harijot Singh Khalsa. Available in audio format at www.sikhnet.com/stories/audio/attitude-gratitude.

34. Jim Wallis, "Steps of Gratitude," *Sojourners*, February, 2016. Reprinted with permission from *Sojourners*, www.sojo.net.

35. Bishop James E. Walsh, MM, "Shine On, Farmer Boy," *Maryknoll Magazine*, July 1980.

36. J. K. Rowling, "I Will Treasure Your Letter," from *Letters of Note*, Thursday, July 14, 2011, www.lettersofnote.com. Reprinted by permission of The Blair Partnership, London, UK.

37. Joan Chittister, "An Alleluia Heart," from *The Breath of the Soul:*

Reflections on Prayer. New London, CT: Twenty-Third Publications, 2009. Copyright © 2009 by Joan Chittister. Used with permission.

38. William J. O'Malley, "Six Inches Off the Ground," from *You'll Never Be Younger: A Good News Spirituality for Those Over 60.* Maryknoll, NY: Orbis Books, 2015.

39. Jeremy Adam Smith, "Six Habits of Highly Grateful People," from *Greater Good*, the online magazine of the Greater Good Science Center, UC Berkeley, November 20, 2013, www.greatergood.berkeley.edu.

40. Thich Nhat Hanh, "A Tangerine Party," from *The Heart of Understanding: Commentaries on the Prajnaparamita Heart Sutra.* Revised Edition. Berkeley, CA: Parallax Press, 2009. Copyright © 2009 by the Unified Buddhist Church.

41. Michael Leach, "The Buddha Who Lives in Our Backyard," from *National Catholic Reporter*, October 22, 2016.

42. Helen Grace Lescheid, "Attitude of Gratitude," from *Thoughts About God,* www.thoughts-about-god.com. Used by permission of the author.

43. Mike Ghouse, "Interfaith Thangsgiving: A Story of Gratitude and Self-Balancing Acts," *The Huffington Post,* November 21, 2012, www.huffingtonpost.com.

44. Mother Mary Joseph Rogers, MM, "Let Us Be Grateful," excerpt from Mother Mary Joseph's Occasional Conferences, August 23, 1929. Used by permission of the Maryknoll Sisters.

45. Mary Beth Werdel, "Praying as a Parent," from *America Magazine*, February 15, 2016.

46. David Steindl-Rast, "Awake, Aware, and Alert," originally appeared in Summer 2001, www.beliefnet.com.

INDEX OF CONTRIBUTORS

Index of Contributors

Frank J. Cunningham is a former newspaper and magazine writer and editor, university writing instructor, and book editor and publisher of Ave Maria Press, Notre Dame, IN **20**

Meister Eckhart was a thirteenth–fourteenth century philosopher, theologian, and mystic. His "nondual Christianity" emphasized both God's immanence and transcendence ....**Last Word**

Mike Ghouse is a motivational speaker, author, and expert on pluralism, Islam, and interfaith issues. He is also a frequent television commentator on politics and foreign policy **43**

Adam Hoffman is an editorial assistant at *Greater Good* magazine . **18**

Terrance W. Klein is a priest serving in the diocese of Dodge City. He is the author of *Vanity Faith* and is a frequent contributor to *America* magazine **27**

Jack Kornfield teaches meditation internationally since 1974 and is one of the key teachers to introduce Buddhist mindfulness practice to the West. Trained as a Buddhist monk, he holds a Ph.D. in clinical psychology and has taught in centers and universities worldwide. His most recent book is *Bringing Home the Dharma: Awakening Right Where You Are* **7**

Anne Lamott is an American poet, essayist, and novelist. She is the author of the *New York Times* bestsellers *Grace (Eventually)*, *Plan B*, *Traveling Mercies*, and *Operating Instructions*, as well as seven novels, including *Rosie* and *Crooked Little Heart* **21**

Michael Leach is publisher emeritus and editor-at-large of Orbis Books. Honored by the Catholic Book Publishers Association with a Lifetime Achievement Award in 2007, he was dubbed "the dean of Catholic book publishing" by *U.S. Catholic* magazine, and has authored or edited several books of his own, including the bestseller *I Like Being Catholic*, *A Maryknoll Book of Prayer*, *The People's Catechism*, and *I Like Being Married* **41**

Helen Grace Lescheid is a spiritual writer and public speaker. She is a regular contributor to *Daily Guideposts, Rejoice!* and *TruthMedia,*

Index of Contributors

THE WAY OF GRATITUDE